Institute of EU Studies, HUFS
New Social Contract ◆ Humanities and Social Science Book Series 05

STAGES OF EUROPEAN INTEGRATION

The Treaties of the European Union
from a Political-Economic Perspective

Institute of EU Studies, HUFS
New Social Contract • Humanities and Social Science Book Series 05

STAGES OF EUROPEAN INTEGRATION

The Treaties of the European Union from a Political-Economic Perspective

Ralf Havertz

HU:iNE

This work was supported by the National Research Foundation of Korea Grant funded by the Korean Government(NRF-2022S1A5C2A02091292)

PREFACE

The treaties of the European Union (EU) are documents of outstanding significance for the process of European integration. With each treaty this process became wider and deeper in the sense that more policy fields were included and the complexity of the legal framework increased. In the early years, when the Treaty of Paris (1952) and the Treaty of Rome (1958) came into force, it was primarily a process of economic integration. But with the following treaties the character of the EU as a political union became more pronounced. Economic and political considerations played a crucial role in this process at all times. Hence, it appeared worthwhile to analyze the legal texts and the historical circumstances in which they were negotiated and adopted from a political-economic point of view. An approach that focuses on the interconnectedness of the evolving institutional framework of the EU, the historical-political conditions for the adoption of each treaty and the economic policies and regulations that were implemented as a result of these agreements promises to provide insights that further a deeper understanding of the different dimensions of the integration process. This approach is complemented by an analysis of the ideological foundations for the negotiation and adoption of these treaties in their different political-economic environments.

Some of the chapters assembled in this book were published as articles in academic journals, but there are also a few new chapters that were not published before. For each of the European treaties there is one chapter that covers its major political-economic aspects and to some extent also the institutional changes that were ushered in with each of the agreements. Attempts at deepening European integration through bold reforms were sometimes hampered by member states who gave priority to the protection of their national interests. At other times fast movements forward were possible, for instance, with the adoption of the common currency, the euro, in 1999 and the admission of ten new member states in 2004, most of which were Central and Eastern European countries. The question is today whether the integration process can advance any further, especially in the fields of social and fiscal policy, and in foreign and defense policy, and if this could eventually lead to the creation of a European federation. Chapter 8 of this book may provide some hints for the future direction of European integration.

The research in this book was conducted in collaboration with the Institute of EU Studies of Hankuk University of Foreign Studies in Seoul and with support of the National Research Foundation of the Republic of Korea. I am very grateful to both institutions for providing me with the opportunity to carry out this research. I hope that reading this book will benefit students of European integration and maybe also readers from the general public who are interested in the development and functioning of the EU. The EU is after all an amazing project that facilitated peace and prosperity for its members over a period of more than seven decades. It is due to the economic and political integration among former adversaries that the region was able to experience the longest period of sustained peace in its history. One of the fascinating characteristics of the EU is the freedom of movement for goods, services, capital, and people that it provides for all citizens of the region. These freedoms create opportunities for the mobility and personal development of European citizens. However, the EU is also about regulations and restrictions, for instance, when it comes to ensuring conditions of fair competition throughout the whole bloc or the curtailing of monopolies. A major insight of this book is that certain freedoms can only be enjoyed in Europe due to the presence of a well-established institutional and regulatory framework. The foundation for this framework was laid by the treaties of the EU.

Daegu, November 2024
Ralf Havertz

Table of Contents

Chapter 1

Introduction
Stages of European Integration

European integration is a gradual process, and the European treaties have played a crucial role in advancing it. With each of the treaties that was concluded by the states of the European Community/the European Union (EC/EU) between 1951 and 2007, this process has deepened, bringing it up to a higher stage of regional integration. With each step, this bloc of states has also moved further forward from a mere international organization, i.e. a confederation, in the direction of a federation. With each treaty, more policy areas have been covered and thus partially or fully shifted from the area of responsibility of the individual states to that of the EU. This has resulted in a very complex set of treaties which together almost, but still incompletely, fulfil the function of a European constitution. Despite the many advances that the EU has made in this process over the years, it has not yet reached the level of a European state. It has given itself an institutional structure which is, as EU Commission President Jose Manuel Barroso (2007) once noted, unique in the world, and as such lies somewhere between a confederation and a federation.

The book traces the changes that have occurred in the EU from treaty to treaty. This involves the institutional changes which these treaties brought about. It is interested in the historical and political-economic conditions for the conclusion of the individual treaties and how these conditions were affected by the implementation of those agreements. The focus here is particularly on the ideological foundations of the treaties. In chapters 2 and 3 of this book, an attempt is made to investigate how functionalism, Keynesianism, statist dirigisme, ordoliberalism and neoliberalism affected these legal texts. All of these ideological approaches had some influence in this process of regional integration in Europe at different points of time. Recently, the focus on ideational influences of European integration was very much on ordoliberalism (Bonefeld 2019; Havertz 2020; Nedergaard 2013, 2019; Hien and Joerges, 2018). The influences of this ideological approach reach far beyond the formation of the *social market economy* in Germany in the first decades after the Second World War. With its focus on the need for a robust regulatory state and the provision of a competitive market across European boundaries, including the prevention of monopolies, the influence of ordoliberalism has been felt in the whole of the EU. This also pertains to the monetary policies of the EU with the European Central Bank (ECB), as an institution that concentrates on monetary stability at its center. Ordoliberal principles provided the economic framework for the economic integration of the EU.

But it was not ordoliberalism alone which can be referenced as an ideational influence on the process of European integration. Keynesianism had an effect on European integration by promoting public spending and state intervention, which aided in the creation of social programs and welfare policies in member nations, particularly during the reconstruction phase after the Second World War. Especially in France, the statist policies of dirigisme encouraged a coordinated approach to economic planning and development, which impacted the early industrial and agricultural policies of the European Economic Community

(EEC) (Warlouzet 2019). Other ideational influences such as neoliberalism, with its promotion of deregulation, privatization, and the free market, could be felt in later periods of this integration process. This especially concerns the Single European Act (SEA) of 1986 and the Maastricht Treaty of 1992, which facilitated the creation of the single market and the euro.

Early on, functionalism, or neo-functionalism had become the leading theory of European integration (Haas 1958). It is still influential today. Neo-functionalism fostered the notion that collaboration in certain industries (such as steel and coal in the Treaty of Paris) would have a spill-over effect and lead to integration in other sectors of the European economy and thus result in deeper political and economic integration, which would in turn promote further European integration.

There, of course, have been differences in the strengths of the influences which these ideologies had on the integration process over time. The analyst of these developments may understand these differences better when viewing them against their changing historical backdrops. In the aftermath of the Second World War, European nations signed the 1951 Treaty of Paris in an attempt to avert future hostilities by cooperating economically and to rebuild their economies by combining their supplies of steel and coal (Fontaine 2000). During the Cold War, Western European nations signed the 1957 Treaty of Rome in an effort to fortify their economic links and create the EEC in order to create a unified front against their communist adversary, the Soviet Bloc, in Central and Eastern Europe (Kramer 1999). At a time when globalization and neoliberalism were on the rise, the SEA was signed, indicating a goal to boost competitiveness by establishing a single market with unrestricted movement of capital, people, products, and services. With the end of the Cold War, European countries responded to the quick changes that were happening at the time and signed the Maastricht Treaty (1992) in an effort to further their political and economic union. This marked the beginning of the European Union (EU) and laid the groundwork for the common European currency, the euro, which was established in 1999. During a period of continuous globalization, the Treaties of Amsterdam (1997) and Nice (2001) were signed, with an emphasis on institutional reforms to get ready for the enlargement of the EU, that involved the accession of ten new member countries in 2004. These treaties also focused on improving cooperation in the fields of justice and foreign policy. After the proposed European Constitution failed, the Treaty of Lisbon (2007) was signed with the aim of tackling the difficulties provided by globalization and guaranteeing the EU's ability to operate with a larger membership.

When analyzing the process of European integration, we need to realize that some countries played a more significant role in promoting it than others. The founding members of the European Communities – Belgium, France, Germany, Italy, Luxembourg, and the Netherlands – laid the groundwork for the gradual process of integration in the EC/EU. As the leading tandem in this process, France and Germany drove it forward, working together to find common ground between German support for budgetary restraint and economic liberalization and French inclinations for sovereignty and state intervention (Warlouzet 2019). As seen by its support for the Common Agricultural Policy (CAP), France played a significant role in European integration by promoting a strong, centralized approach to economic planning and the adoption of common policies. Germany, on the other hand, supported ordoliberal ideas, which placed a heavy emphasis on fiscal restraint, a stable regulatory framework, and maintaining competition inside the EU (Havertz 2020; Warlouzet 2019). The country also significantly influenced the design of the Economic and Monetary Union (EMU) of the EU, which involved the establishment of the euro. In this process Germany insisted on the ECB's focus on fiscal responsibility and price stability.

> Germany largely succeeded in uploading its stability culture to the European level. Indeed, EMU's crucial design features such as the Maastricht criteria, the independence of the European Central Bank (ECB), the prohibition of monetary financing, the ECB's primary focus on price stability, the no-bailout clause and the SGP all result from German demands. (Schoeller and Heidebrecht 2024, 2512)

The United Kingdom which joined the EC in 1973 is not a member anymore after it left the bloc in 2020. The United Kingdom has both promoted and stalled the process of economic integration. The country favored the liberalization of trade and services in the EU and supported the growth of the single market. But it also opted-out from crucial developments such as the free movement of people within the bloc that was initiated with the Schengen Agreement and the establishment of the common currency. Despite being a full member of the EU, the country regularly claimed a "special status" for itself in the bloc (Her Majesty's Government 2016). In contrast to other member states' aspirations for a closer political union, the British approach to integration frequently prioritized economic cooperation over political integration.

After several rounds of new admissions, the largest round occurred in 2004 with many countries from Central and Eastern Europe joining the EU. This highlighted the EU's role in promoting economic growth and post-Cold War reconciliation. The EU's institutional ability to handle such diversity was called into question by the admission of these new members, which sparked discussions about possible boundaries to further enlargement, particularly with reference to Turkey and the Western Balkans (Devrim and Schulz 2009). The EU's geopolitical position was strengthened as an outcome of the enlargement process, but it also resulted in increasing disparities in the economic development across the region and differences in political development, with countries such as Hungary and (temporarily) also Poland backsliding on their democratization (Sedelmeier 2024). This together with the increasing focus of some member states on their national interests has made it more difficult for the EU to agree on important issues.

The book is primarily interested in the political-economic foundations of European unification and the conditions that gave rise to them. In this sense, the book should not be understood as a comprehensive commentary on the treaties, but as a reflection of the political-economic conditions in which they were concluded and implemented. The reader may note that some of the European treaties were more consequential than others in that they had a greater impact on either the institutional structure or the functioning of the economy, especially with the creation of the single market, which is still a work in progress and will remain so for the foreseeable future (ERT 2024). The treaties that were most consequential are the Treaty of Rome, which resulted in the formation of the EEC, the Treaty of Maastricht which is the foundational document for the EU, and the Lisbon Treaty, which expanded the competence of the EU in some crucial policy fields, especially in the area of foreign and security policy. But the other treaties are also worth analyzing, because each of them spawned some developments that involved significant changes to the ways in which the EU functions.

In the following, I will give an overview over the individual chapters of this book, each of which covers one of the treaties of the EC/EU. The chapters are ordered chronologically, starting with the Treaty of Paris from 1951 and ending with the Treaty of Lisbon of 2007. This approach allows the reader to follow some of the major institutional and political-economic developments in this bloc as they have unfolded over time. The Constitutional Treaty of 2004 was excluded as a topic of analysis from this book since it did not come into force after it was rejected in two referenda in France and the Netherlands.

The first significant step of European integration was made with the Treaty of Paris which established the European Coal and Steel Community (ECSC). Chapter 2 investigates how this first EC fostered supranational cooperation and interdependence among its member states and thus favored collaboration over rivalry. It highlights the importance of this treaty for creating the first supranational treaty organization in history and the first international anti-cartel authority as well. This chapter also outlines the organizational structure of this first EC with its main institutions such as the High Authority which laid the groundwork for the next step of integration that was gone with the Treaties of Rome in 1957.

Chapter 3 covers the Treaty of Rome of 1957 and discusses the influence of ordoliberal principles on competition and social policy. It looks at the ordoliberal underpinnings of European integration and makes the case that these principles had a significant influence on the process of economic integration, especially when it comes to the establishment of an economic order framework. For the purpose of analyzing how ordoliberal concepts affected European integration – particularly competition law and social policy – the study draws on the work of Peter Nedergaard (2013; 2019) and others. The chapter considers how ordoliberalism has influenced European economic and social integration over the long run and how it affected the EU's approach to economic governance.

Chapter 4 describes the slowdown in European integration during the mid-1960s to early 1980s, followed by the revitalization efforts of the SEA in 1986, which aimed to complete the Single European Market (SEM). The treaty attempted to revive this process by enacting significant institutional changes. These included granting the European Parliament more authority, formally recognizing the European Council, and changing the voting process in the Council of Ministers to qualified majority voting (QMV) in some policy fields. The principal aim of the SEA was to finalize the SEM by guaranteeing the unrestricted movement of capital, products, people, and services by the end of 1992.

A significant step toward European economic integration was taken with the 1992 Maastricht Treaty, which founded the EU and prepared the introduction of the euro. This treaty is at the focus of chapter 5 of this book. The treaty created the European Central Bank (ECB) to regulate monetary policy and prevented member states from pursuing their own independent policy in this field. The inability of member states to react independently to economic shocks became an issue during the euro crisis, particularly for Greece. The Economic and Monetary Union's (EMU) rigorous separation of monetary and fiscal policies was one of the fundamental faults exposed by this crisis. Since then position papers from the Juncker Commission, which this chapter reflects on, have bolstered calls for closer fiscal integration inside the EU. The adoption of a sizable relief fund in response to the Covid-19 crisis during EU Commission President Ursula von der Leyen's administration is taken as evidence that fiscal integration on a European level is feasible. Achieving future fiscal and monetary policy convergence is seen as crucial to the EU's political unification.

Chapter 6 treats the Treaty of Amsterdam of 1997, which reformed EU institutions and decision-making processes and was supposed to prepare for a significant round of enlargement. The treaty strengthened the roles of the European Parliament and the Court of Justice, further expanded the use of QMV in the Council, and introduced changes in several policy fields, including justice, home affairs, foreign policy, and fundamental rights. It also introduced the option for closer cooperation among member states in specific policy areas. This treaty was not as transformative or controversial as the preceding Maastricht Treaty and the SEA. The chapter highlights how the treaty also fell short of the expectations concerning the preparation of the bloc for the accession of a larger number of Central and Eastern European countries. It, furthermore, stresses that the Treaty of Amsterdam, despite its shortcomings, brought about some important institutional and procedural adjustments that supported further economic integration within the EU.

The Treaty of Nice is treated in chapter 7 of this book. It was signed in 2001 and became effective in 2003 with the goal of reforming the EU's institutions and decision-making procedures to accommodate the enlargement of 2004 when ten new member states (NMS) joined the EU and expanded its size from 15 to 25 members. This reform involved the redistribution of voting rights in the Council of the EU, which favored larger countries such as Germany and France. The chapter examines the economic and social impacts of the integration of the NMS. In doing so it concentrates on trade growth, migration trends, and economic development. Whereas the integration of these NMS has frequently been described as a success, the chapter also points to problems that came up with the enlargement such as the imbalance between the huge benefits reaped in this process by the old member countries (OMS) compared to the smaller gains in the NMS. It also points to concerns over the NMS's deindustrialization and their function as a pool of inexpensive labor for the OMS. The chapter attempts to provide more clarity on these contrasting viewpoints.

Chapter 8 explores the Treaty of Lisbon, signed in 2007, which further advanced political integration but fell short of creating a federation. The treaty introduced the High Representative of the Union for Foreign Affairs and Security Policy – the foreign minister of the EU – and the President of the European Council. It advanced political integration and brought the EU closer to a political union, but did not live up to the hopes of cosmopolitan and federalist intellectuals such as Jürgen Habermas, who pushed for a more forceful move toward a supranational democracy on European level. The chapter discusses Habermas's views on European integration, his advocacy for a European constitution, his claim of a need for the creation of a European public sphere, and the critique of his vision in the context of globalization and neoliberal capitalism.

The conclusion reflects on the advances in the process of European economic integration that were made with each treaty and also on the shortcomings of the treaties in the facilitation of this process. This last chapter also involves considerations on the future of the integration process and possible developments in it that may bring it closer to the completion of the project of a political union in Europe.

Chapter 2

Supranationalism and Interdependence in Europe

The Case of the European Coal and Steel Community

Introduction

The establishment of the European Coal and Steel Community (ECSC) has been a groundbreaking development, because it was the first decisive step toward European integration and realigned power constellations in Europe. Both were important prerequisites for the achievement of Europe's long-term objectives of peace and prosperity, goals which Robert Schuman (2010) emphasized in this historic declaration of 9 May 1950, when he first proposed the creation of the ECSC. His declaration was drafted by Jean Monnet, who can be considered the key figure in advancing European integration in its early stages (Piodi 2010; Ver Loren van Themaat 1994).

There are two notable things which the ECSC did first: It was the world's first to establish a supranational treaty organization and the first to create an international anti-cartel authority. This study will focus on supranationalism as a theoretical and institutional framework for safeguarding peace and prosperity in Europe and show how the interdependence among the members of the ECSC which was facilitated by supranationalism increased their drive toward cooperation.

The new institutions that were built to govern the ECSC provided a blueprint for the core institutions of the European Union (EU) as we know them today: The European Council, the European Commission, the European Parliament, and the European Court of Justice (Archer 2000, 39). The ECSC also provided a framework for the further integration process of the European Communities, because the Treaties of Rome that were signed in 1957 and established the European Economic Community (EEC) and the European Atomic Energy Community (Euratom) were largely based on the structure that had already been created by the ECSC.

This study starts with a reflection on the theory of supranationalism. This will be followed by theoretical considerations about the *structures of interdependence* and an attempt to place it in an international relations framework. The hypothesis of this study is that it was interdependence and the absolute gains that sprung from it which increased the further drive toward European integration. Supranationalism was the crucial organizational element which made these structures of interdependence highly complex and engendered the entanglement of ECSC members and their interests in a way that cooperation was seen as mutually beneficial and in common interest, and preferable to competition. In this context the international relations theories of neo-realism (Waltz 1959) and neo-liberalism (Koehane and Nye 1977; Koehane 1989) will be discussed and it will be argued that the process of European integration provides evidence that supports the neo-liberal view.

It will then focus on the importance of the Schuman Declaration for the process of European integration. This will be followed by an account of the contribution which individuals such as Robert Schuman, Jean Monnet, and Konrad Adenauer made to this process. In the next step, the institutional framework of the ECSC will be examined, and it will be shown in what way this community already anticipated the later institutional structure of the EU. Throughout this study it will be analyzed how the ECSC contributed to securing peace and prosperity in Europe as the two main goals of this treaty organization. In this context, it is noteworthy that the ECSC managed to promote peaceful relations among European countries by focusing on the creation of economic opportunities and growth for all countries involved. In its beginnings, the primary focus of integration was on economic development and reconstruction, and peace was seen as a welcome by-product (Moravcsik 2013; Milward 1984; Scheingold 1971).

In comparison to the later comprehensive progress in European integration, the ECSC may appear only as a small step. However, it was the first crucial step in this process without which the following steps would have been much more difficult, if at all possible. The study concludes with an appraisal of the overall achievements of the ECSC and its contributions to the creation of the EU.

Supranationalism

It is not exactly known who was the first to introduce the term "supranationalism" in the literature. But it is clear that Albert Einstein was one of the first to enthusiastically embrace the term, when he suggested in *The Atlantic Monthly* to establish an international regime tasked with the "supranational control of atomic energy" (Einstein 1947). He made that proposal against the backdrop of the Cold War. According to Einstein, giving up national control of atomic energy and putting it in the hands of a global authority would be the best way to prevent nuclear war in the future. This shift of sovereignty from national to supranational level would constitute the first step toward the creation of a "world government", the establishment of which he predicted as something inevitable (ibid.).[1] These words of Einstein show that, from the beginning, supranationalism was conceived as a means to secure peace by shifting national sovereignty in areas crucial for the maintenance of peace to a new level of government that was supposed to be created above the level of the state as principle actor in international relations, thus, questioning the central position of the state in the international system. When the treaty of the ECSC was signed on 18 April 1951, it emphasized the supranational character of the organization explicitly in its Article 9 on the High Authority, the governing body of the ECSC, where it delineated the supranational powers of the High Authority and asked all member states to respect the supranational character of the ECSC (ECSC, Art. 9).

European history after the Second World War shows that supranationalism was key in bringing European nations together by generating common interests that were stronger than their national interests. Put differently: In the process of European integration, it increasingly was in European countries' national interest to focus on common interests. Supranationalism involves the creation of new overarching interests, that would not exist or at least not exist to the same extent in an exclusively intergovernmental context or in that of an international organization. Supranationalism was the key for the lasting peace in Europe since

1 Einstein had already supported the idea of a "world government" in November 1945 in an article for *The Atlantic Quarterly*, where he reacted to the first use of atomic bombs in warfare in human history by the American government in Hiroshima and Nagasaki (Calaprice, Kennefick, and Schulmann 2015, p. 257)

the Second World War. It helped to temper nationalism and the tribal grievances of individual nation-states. It provided the ideal framework for states to work out their differences peacefully and work toward compromise and consensus.

The main supranational institution of the ECSC was the High Authority which had "some very important exclusive powers" (Groenendijk and Hospers 2002, p. 605). But it's noteworthy that the ECSC was not purely supranational. With the Council of Ministers, it also had a strong intergovernmental body which the High Authority had to cooperate with and which served as a liaison between the High Authority and the governments of the six nations that participated in the ECSC. We will return to the institutional structure of the ECSC below.

Supranationalism as theoretical and institutional framework distinguishes European integration from all other forms of international cooperation. Its progressive growth necessarily results in the weakening of the nation-states that are members of the supranational structure and in the strengthening of the latter. It can be expected that at some point of time the quality of cooperation and the institutional framework that keeps it together will change and transform the group of nation-states into a new state.

With the ECSC, the first supranational treaty organization was brought to life in 1952, when the treaty came into effect. The scope of the sovereignty that was passed from the members states to the supranational level of that organization was limited, but with coal and steel it happened in a field that was significant for the economies of France and Germany, the two largest member states at the center of this first European Community. It was the ingeniousness and visionary approach of Jean Monnet and Robert Schuman to start European integration in a field that was vital for the member states, promised to deliver some concrete economic results, and facilitate peace at the same time.

Supranationalism and Interdependence

From the beginning of supranationalism one of the core elements of this approach to securing international peace was interdependence. With the foundation of the EU, there is historical evidence now for the fact that the creation of supranational structures is better suited for the establishment of a stable relationship among states than mere intergovernmental arrangements. The reason for this conclusion is that the interdependence which European integration generated among the member states, first, of the European Communities, and later, of the EU, is a much deeper one than could ever be engendered by intergovernmental cooperation among states.

In their seminal work on *Power and Interdependence* Robert Koehane and Joseph Nye (1977, p. 26) referred to a number of organizations as facilitators of interdependence in international relations: The Organization of Economic Cooperation and Development (OECD), the General Agreement on Tariffs and Trade (GATT), the International Monetary Fund (IMF), and the European Community. However, they did not distinguish between the intergovernmental and supranational features of these organizations and treated them all as institutions that developed "extensive consultative arrangements" (ibid.). In this context, Koehane and Nye did not address an important aspect that distinguishes the first three organizations from the European Community: The supranational element in the organization of the European Community and later the EU, which involved a deeper and more complex form of interdependence than was given with the cooperation in the intergovernmental framework of the other organizations.

Koehane and Nye (1977, p. 25) emphasized that international relations have become more complex with the creation of these institutions. In addition to the interstate channels of interaction, new – transgovernmental and transnational – ties have emerged. Their term "transgovernmental" actually comes relatively close to supranational, but "transgovernmental" is ambiguous because it may at the same time also refer to the intergovernmental cooperation among states. They made an important point when they stressed that interaction among states has moved far beyond the realist paradigm that perceives it as confined to interstate relations.

In the book *Power and Interdependence* Koehane and Nye (1977, pp. 24-26) introduced their concept of complex interdependence which has three main characteristics: 1. Multiple channels connect societies across borders; the ties can exist between governments and nongovernmental actors, especially elites, on both sides of a border; they can be either formal or informal. 2. Issues in relations among states "are not arranged in a clear or consistent hierarchy [...] which means that military security does not consistently dominate the agenda" (ibid., p. 25). 3. Complex interdependence precludes the use of military force by one government against another government that is part of the interdependent structure. On closer examination, it becomes clear that the ECSC from its beginning involved elements of complex interdependence. One could argue that it was set up precisely for the purpose of establishing a structure that conforms to this concept, even though the term itself was not yet known at the time.

Koehane and Nye criticized the traditional realist and the neorealist schools for their limited view of international relations as competition among states for relative gains. The neorealist theorist Kenneth N. Waltz (1959) famously assumed that in the international system, the state would be the primary actor, and in the absence of any overarching authority one would have to assume anarchy as the primary condition among the states in that system. Koehane (1989, p. 10) objected to these ideas and argued – with explicit reference to the European Community – that they become "theoretically implausible when applied to situations in which substantial mutual gains can be realized through cooperation and in which governments do not expect others to threaten them with force." This is precisely the case with European integration and its focus on supranationalism, which focused on the pursuit of mutual gains by a supranational authority. When the ECSC was created, the trust in the ability of the High Authority to generate such mutual gains was so strong that all member countries were ready to give up some of their sovereign powers of government in order to create that institution.

Supranational Elements of the Schuman Declaration

The text of the Schuman Declaration was drafted by Monnet. As the mythical narrative of European Integration has it, he made the notes for this declaration on a hiking tour in the Swiss Alps, where the reclusive atmosphere helped him to see European development in its broader context and generate a vision of an integrated Europe (Chira-Pascanut 2014, p. 1242).

When Robert Schuman, who had served as prime minister of France and who was foreign minister of France at the time, gave his speech on European construction on 9 May 1950, it was not the first time that the idea of pooling the production of French and German coal and steel was pronounced. Such ideas were in circulation at least since the mid-1920s, when the International Steel Cartel was established. But it was the timing which made the difference with Schuman's proposal and allowed his plan to become reality (Burgess 2011, p. 6). Germany was weakened due to the destructions of the war, and the French steel industry was in urgent need of cooking coal which the Ruhr area held in abundance (Berger 2013, p. 68).

Schuman suggested to place both coal and steel under a common authority and open it for other European participants. This was a proposal addressed primarily to France, Germany and the Benelux states (Belgium, The Netherlands, and Luxembourg),[2] because this is the geographic area where the production of coal and steel was concentrated. What Schuman was proposing was nothing less than the world's first supranational treaty organization. He suggested that both countries France and Germany give up their sovereignty in the crucial area of coal and steel production and place it "in the hands of a common High Authority" (Schuman 2010, p. 7).

After two wars that were started by Germany in the first half of the 20th century, Monnet and Schuman had realized that long-term peace in Europe could only be achieved, if Germany was firmly integrated within a larger international structure. The ECSC was supposed to provide the framework for this firm inclusion. With its focus on coal and steel it targeted the German capacity of weapons production which at the time was concentrated in the Ruhr area. Coal and Steel were the indispensable raw materials for the production of ammunitions of war. The French expected that the merging of coal and steel production would render war between France and Germany "not only unthinkable but also impossible" (ibid.). "The Schuman Plan was designed to alleviate concerns that Germany's dominance in coal and steel could be used to harm European construction efforts or to build another war machine." (Alter and Steinberg 2007, p. 2) A new war in Europe that would originate from West Germany was not immi-

2 These states were not explicitly mentioned in the Schuman Declaration.

nent at the time, it was not an immediate threat. But war between Germany and France was a recurring pattern over the course of almost a century, so something had to be done to break this pattern (Calingaert 1996, p. 97).

During the U.S. occupation of Germany, the occupation authorities focused on the deconcentration of the Ruhr steel firms. Deconcentration is also what the ECSC tried to achieve. This is where American influence on the European integration process was of particular importance. It resulted in the inclusion of the anti-trust provisions of Articles 65 and 66 of the Treaty of Paris (Martin 2004). Article 65 prohibits the creation of trusts that would undermine competition. Under Article 65 any price fixing, any undermining or restriction of the production of coal and steel, and any creation of market divisions was forbidden (ECSC, Art 65, 1). Any violation of these prohibitions could be punished with draconic fines of up to the double of a company's turnover (ECSC, Art 65, 5).

Integrating Germany meant creating mutual interests of France and Germany, interests which superseded national interests; and these interests had to be political *and* economic in nature. They had to be strong enough to make both states dependent on the newly created supranational structures. Integrating Germany also meant that Germany would be prevented from using its dominance in the market for steel and its vast reservoirs of coal in the Ruhr area to gain advantage over its neighbors to the West and prevent it from impeding the reconstruction of the industries and economies in these countries (ibid., p. 3).

Monnet and Schuman recognized that securing peace and increasing prosperity could be two mutually reinforcing goals. A peace that was accompanied by economic prosperity was more likely to be a lasting peace than one not supported by economic growth. The pooling of raw materials as vital as coal and steel could therefore be the ideal means to reach both goals at the same time. At the center of Schuman's proposal was the idea that peace in Europe could only be achieved, if European countries focus more on cooperation than on competition. This included the modernization and improvement of the production of the coal and steel industries in all countries involved. Coal and steel were to be supplied on identical terms in all member countries of the new supranational structure; and the living conditions of the workers in these industries equalized (ibid., p. 8), which shows that the ECSC already was designed to have a social dimension.

There has been a (now historical) debate in the literature about the main motive for European integration in the ECSC. The central question of this debate was whether economic or geopolitical factors were more important for that process. According to Moravcsik (2013, p. 776), there is broad scholarly agreement in historiographical research "to stress economic factors as most important, but also to include geopolitics alongside them." In absence of a real peace treaty, the Schuman Plan served as a substitute for such a treaty. With its focus on economic cooperation the ECSC can be understood as "economic peace treaty" (Milward 1984, p. 475), or as Holland (1993, p. 6) put it: the ECSC can be considered as "Europe's first peace movement." Scheingold (1971, pp. 378-379) also stressed the significance of the economic motive for the creation of the ECSC: "Their goal was not simply to utilize integration as agent of economic reconstruction, but also to exploit a single continent-sized market to increase the rate of economic growth which had sagged badly during the interwar period – particularly in relation to the United States."

The Schuman declaration included the vision of a "united Europe" (Schuman 2010, p. 7). It was clear that many further steps had to follow on the creation of the ECSC before a united Europe could become reality. Schuman hoped that his declaration would lead to "the realization of the first concrete foundation of a European Federation" (ibid., p. 8). Monnet, principal drafter of the declaration, had removed the term supranational from the treaty and replaced it with "federation." Monnet actually confessed in his memoirs that he did not like the term supranationalism (Burgess 2011, p. 9); but that does not change the fact that the supranational character of the ECSC was its decisive and game-changing innovation which laid the foundation for further European integration. The fact that he was not talking about a "confederation" – which would have been an indicator for the intention to establish an *international organization,* not a federation – is telling: The long-term vision of Schuman and Monnet was the creation of a European state, the United States of Europe, with France and Germany at its center and with a power-sharing arrangement between the national level and the European level.

Monnet was a functionalist who tried to use functional integration in selected economic sectors in order to reach his long-term goal of a unified European state. The establishment of the ECSC with its foundation in a functionalist approach also resulted in the generation of a functionalist theory by Ernst Haas, a political scientist at Berkeley. Gillingham (2003, p. 28) commented on Haas' theory: "Functionalism holds that the creation of new institutions at the supranational level will have effects that 'spill over' into the national arena and so generate counterpressures at the supranational level."

Supranationalism was not the sole principle which the ECSC focused on. Its integration process was designed to include a combination of supranational and intergovernmental elements. While supranationalism was strongly pronounced in the Treaty Establishing the ECSC, this principle has later been watered down when the EEC and Euratom were launched. With reference to the ECSC, Haas (1958, pp. 526-527) noted that "supranationality in practice has developed into a hybrid in which neither the federal nor the intergovernmental tendency has clearly triumphed." According to Haas, whether the focus of the European Communities was on supranationalism or intergovernmentalism depended on how intergovernmental powers of the individual nation states made use of their intergovernmental power. It was perfectly possible that a member state would use its intergovernmental powers to pursue common interests and, in a way, strengthen supranationalism.

Early Proponents of Supranationalism in Europe

Originally, pooling the French and German production of coal and steel under a common High Authority was Monnet's idea. He served as Planning Commissioner of France and was responsible for organizing French reconstruction after the Second World War. When he suggested to Schuman to integrate the coal and steel industries of France and Germany, Monnet already had had a long career as businessman and organizer of war supplies during both world wars. In the First World War, he served as inter-allied head of war supplies, and in the Second World War, he became the chairman of the Anglo-French committee for the coordination of war supplies (Piodi 2010, p. 17). This is an interesting detail of Monnet's background: He had a clear idea of the supplies that were necessary to wage war. Which also means that he was aware how war supplies would have to be organized so war was less likely to occur. This especially concerned coal and steel as the basic raw materials of ammunitions of war. If the production of coal and steel were brought under the common control of countries which had historically often been at war with each other, as in the case of France and Germany, it would on both sides be possible to limit the production of weapons or at least commonly control it. Both sides would be aware of the actions of the other and have a say in regard of the production of potential war supplies, respectively.

Monnet was the first president of the High Authority, a role that he took on in August 1952 and filled until May 1955. He was well-suited to fill in this position, not only because of his experience as organizer of war supplies and as Planning Commissioner but also because of his experience as Deputy Secretary-General of the League of Nations. He had a crucial role in the establishment of the League of Nations and served as its deputy head for three years (1920-1923). Which means that he had broad experience in organizing international cooperation. With the new supranational features of the ECSC, cooperation between France, Germany and the other four member countries of the ECSC – The Netherlands, Belgium, Luxembourg, and Italy – occurred on a whole new level – a new development that may only have been possible because of the broad experience of Monnet in international cooperation.

What may have been even more significant is his transatlantic contacts. He was involved in a broad network of powerful people and knew many of the key political figures in the U.S., who promoted the process of European integration and supported Monnet in his plans to go the first steps in European integration in the area of coal and steel (Chira-Pascanut 2014, p. 1243). But it was not only Monnet's power and influence behind the scenes that contributed to the realization of the first European community, it was also his personal and diplomatic competences that allowed him to convince politicians in France of the viability of his plans.

Schuman also had a background that made him an ideal person to think about ways to bring France and Germany together and to prevent future conflict between these two countries. He was born a German citizen with a mother from Luxembourg and a father who came from the Alsace region which was contested between France and Germany for a long time and which today is French territory. In 1912, after getting a law degree in Berlin he opened a law firm in Lorraine, another province that was contested between France and Germany and today is a part of France (Piodi 2010, p. 13). He stayed in Lorraine after the region was annexed by France in 1918 (the official recognition of that annexation followed in 1919 with the Treaty of Versailles). Schuman now became a French citizen. He soon started to get engaged in French politics and became a member of the French National Assembly. Schuman with his broad experience in and understanding of both countries was the ideal person to make a proposal that would bridge the divide between France and Germany and allow both countries to overcome the enmity that had resulted in three devastating wars since 1870.

The ECSC was an exclusively French initiative. However, for the implementation of Schuman's far-reaching proposal, the French government needed German cooperation and found a reliable partner in German chancellor Konrad Adenauer: "Adenauer favored integration to bolster the Western alliance and German security and sided with Jean Monnet against German business and Minister of Economics Ludwig Erhard, both of whom preferred a Free Trade Area." (Moravcsik 2013, pp. 780-781) Adenauer was driven by the motive to improve the subordinate position of his country after the Second World War. He wanted to regain equality with the other states in Western Europe, especially France, so he accepted the plan, despite the resistance to it that existed in his own country (Jovanovic 2005, p. 8) There is evidence that Adenauer supported Franco-German integration as early as 1923 (Berger 2013, p. 74), but it was not him, who suggested this bold move to the French. In fact, with Germany being the cause of two world wars in the first half of the 20th century a German chancellor would have been ill-suited as visionary of European integration.

The High Authority at the Center of the ECSC

With the Treaty of Paris several institutions for the administration of the ECSC were created: The High Authority, the Common Assembly, the Special Council of Ministers, the Court of Justice, and a Consultative Committee. "The Council allowed the member states to contribute to policy-making; the Court interpreted and applied ECSC law; and an Assembly and a Consultative Committee represented party political and sectional interests respectively." (Archer 2000, p. 39) These institutions of the ECSC provided a blueprint for the core institutions of the EU as we know them today: The European Council, the European Commission, the European Parliament, and the European Court of Justice. Some of the functions of these EU institutions had already been anticipated by the institutions of the ECSC. These institutions commenced their operations in the second half of 1952. The High Authority had its inaugural session on 10 August 1952 in Luxembourg. The Special Council of Ministers came together for the first time on 8 September 1952. The first meeting of the Common Assembly of the ECSC was held in Strasbourg on 10 September 1952. It was chaired by Paul-Henri Spaak. The first judges of the Court of Justice were sworn in on 10 December 1952. By the end of 1952, the institutional structure of the ECSC was fully functional.

The High Authority of the ECSC can primarily be understood as a regulatory institution. This is what distinguishes it from today's European Commission. As a regulatory agency it had "vast powers to regulate *inter alia* investments and subsidies, production and prices" (Ver Loren van Themaat 1994). It has been described as an "unprecedented innovation" in international relations "for never before had established states in Europe voluntarily agreed to the joint delegation of part of their national sovereignty to an independent supranational body" (Burgess 2011, p. 10).

It was the primary function of the High Authority to control the production of coal and steel in the common market that was created with the ECSC. The High Authority was also expected to secure unimpeded competition and non-discriminatory behavior of all members states in the area of coal and steel. Even though the members of the High Authority were appointed by the individual member states, they were "independent of their control" (Archer 2000, p. 39). With the creation of the High Authority a new type of governmental structure was born that allowed different states to make decisions commonly without being directly involved in the common decision-making process.

Conclusion

The establishment of the ECSC can be seen as the first move toward cooperation among former archenemies that eventually resulted in a liberal order which replaced the imperialist paradigm that dictated European politics for a long time. The ECSC showed that it is possible for former enemies to come together through the generation of common interests which are stronger than national interests; or, in other words, to create a system in which it is in the vital national interest of all participants to focus on common interests. This could be achieved through the facilitation of intra-European competition. The ECSC resulted in the abolishment of "discriminatory practices in the production, sale, and shipment of coal, iron ore, scrap, and steel" (Grotewold 1973, p. 355), and it is these practical accomplishments that contributed to economic growth in all participating countries and set the stage for further European integration.

The meaning of supranationalism for the process of European integration evolved over time, and with the European Commission and the European Parliament there are now two crucial supranational institutional bodies at the center of the institutional structure of the EU. Historically, there have been shifts in the strength of the focus on supranationalism and intergovernmentalism (Chryssochoou 2001, p. 27), and it appears that supranationalism has recently stagnated in its development. The power of the European Council has considerably increased over the last two decades, even though the European Council's position has been weakened according to European law, which gave new competences to the EP and tried to strengthen democracy in Europe with the Treaty of Amsterdam. Nonetheless, the European Council is the institution which could secure its effectiveness and decision-making powers more decisively than all other institutions of the EU. This can partly be explained by the increasing importance of national interests which the individual member states in the EU are less and less ready to compromise on. The European Council together with the Council of Ministers is the institution that is best suited to pursue these national interests on European level.

A decisive move toward more supranationalism could come with the implementation of recent suggestions by French president Emmanuelle Macron, who proposed the integration of fiscal policy in the EU. This would mean that considerable government authority is transferred from the national to the supranational level. A first step in this direction may be a *euro zone budget*, as agreed between Macron and Angela Merkel at a Franco-German meeting in June 2018 (Carrel and Nienaber 2018). This budget was supposed to be operational until 2021. However, the coronavirus pandemic and the economic crisis which it brought in its wake interfered with these plans. The future will show whether such proposals will be successful. It is important to note that, apparently, it has to be someone from France who is creative enough to generate a vision that would allow the EU to make another comprehensive leap forward in its integration process. Whenever this process makes more progress, supranationalism will be at its center.

Chapter 3

Ordoliberalism as Early Ideational Influence on European Economic Integration

Introduction

European economic integration was an incremental process. The signing of the Treaty of Rome in 1957 was just the starting point of a development which lasted several decades and has only recently been completed. When we refer to the Treaty of Rome as a starting point, this does not mean that the European Coal and Steel Community (ECSC) which was founded in 1952 with the Treaty of Paris had no significance for this integration process. Pooling the production of coal and steel in the six founding states of the European Community can be interpreted as an important first (to some extent preparatory) step for the more comprehensive steps that were taken with the enactment of the Treaty of Rome.[1]

---

1 The Treaty of Rome was not just about economic integration it also included the creation of the European Atomic Energy Community (EAEC), the purpose of which was to secure energy supply throughout the territory of all members states. Back in these days nuclear energy was seen as an important and safe source of energy supply for the future. The environmental perils of this technology were not well known at this point of time. This has changed meanwhile with

This study focuses on the European Economic Community (EEC) and the ordoliberal foundations of European economic integration. Its *main hypothesis* is that ordoliberal principles were guiding the integration process. It assumes that these principles formed the ideational basis of the process that was initiated with the signing of the Treaty of Rome. The ordoliberal element that was at the center of the integration process was a framework order for the economy of the European Community (EC). In many ways the process of European economic integration looks as though it meticulously followed the prescripts of ordoliberal theory. The problem is that there are no official documents or statements from the time when the Treaty of Rome was negotiated that would include any specific references to ordoliberalism or the social market economy as a model for the way economic integration was organized. Until recently, the influence of ordoliberalism on the policy area of competition has primarily been studied through the analysis of interviews that were conducted with some of the founding fathers of the EC and "studies of the negotiations that led to the articles of competition policy in the European Coal and Steel Community" (ECSC) (Nedergaard 2013, pp. 2-3). According to Peter Nedergaard (2019, p. 12), this line of inquiry is based on "more or less well-founded assumptions about such influence." Which is rather dissatisfying and poses a methodological problem for any research that sets out to provide evidence for ideational influences of ordoliberalism on the process of European integration: What evidence can be used to support the main hypothesis of this research? This study adopts a methodological approach advanced by Nedergaard (2013), who suggested that, in absence of any clear evidence in the form of references to ordoliberalism or the social market economy in the

Germany, the economically strongest country of the European Union, phasing out nuclear energy until 2022.

founding documents of the EC, one would have to look at the treaty provisions and the policies flowing from them, and analyze how far they conform to the economic theories that could potentially have had an influence.

Nedergaard (2013) identifies two main policy areas of importance that may have been influenced by ordoliberalism: competition policy and monetary policy. In a later study he added agricultural policy as an area of inquiry (Nedergaard 2019). According to Nedergaard (2013, p. 3), "influence has to be measured on the backdrop of a detailed specification of the characteristics of ordoliberalism itself compared to the strongest ideational alternatives." Following this methodological approach, the potential alternative ideational influences on competition policy and social policy, the two policy areas which this study is focusing on, would have to be determined. As potential alternative influences to ordoliberalism on competition policy one may distinguish between laissez-faire liberalism (or neoliberalism) and French interventionism (or dirigisme). The main candidates for influence on social policy other than ordoliberalism would again be laissez-faire liberalism and French dirigisme; the latter can largely be described as Keynesian in nature. Since monetary policy did not play an important role when the EEC was launched, this study will neglect monetary policy and focus on competition policy and social policy.

Competition policy is of eminent interest for this study, because in the early days of European integration, the focus was primarily on the establishment of an order that would allow participants in the European market to act uninhibited by both economic power in the form of monopolies and governments imposing their agendas on the community. According to Jörges and Rödl (2004, p. 5), the Treaty of Rome was meant to open up national economies and guarantee "anti-discrimination rules and the commitment to a system of undistorted competition." This was a process which took on steam especially with the launch of the Single Market Program of the EC. Accordingly, during the 1980s and in the time that followed, competition law gained in importance and is seen by many as a center-piece of EU regulation. Gillingham (2003, p. 250) talked about "the rise of competition law within the Community" which was "inextricably bound up with the 1980s process of globalization, the institution of domestic competition regimes, and the spread of neoliberalism." According to Wilks and McGowan (1996, p. 226), until the 1990s, competition policy advanced to a status that took "pre-eminence over other areas of Community law."

The social policy of the EU also had its beginnings in the EEC. In the Treaty of Rome there is a larger section on social policy under title III in articles 117 to 128.[2] The Treaty of Rome has often been celebrated as the foundation of social policy in the EU, because it includes the creation of the European Social Fund (articles 123 to 127). However, over time social policy turned out the be a policy area of minor importance for the Union. This study assumes that the low salience which social policy has for the EU today can be traced back to its beginnings in the Treaty of Rome, where provisions of social policy were codified for the first time in the context of European integration. It is noteworthy that providing evidence for an ideational influence of ordoliberalism on social policy is somewhat more of a challenge than showing that there was such an influence on competition policy. This is due to the fact that competition policy came to play an important role in the regulatory policies of the EU, while social policy appears to have been of much lower concern for the Union.

Why were these two policy areas chosen to be investigated in this study? The framework order can be considered as the core

2 The *Consolidated Version of the Treaty on the Functioning of the European Union* (2012) lists these articles in an amended and revised version under title X, articles 151 to 164.

element of ordoliberal prescriptions for the organization of an economy; and competition policy is at the heart of the ordoliberal attempt to establish a free-market economy based on that order. Social policy was chosen because the establishment of a framework order according to ordoliberal principles can be expected to have consequences for social policy. There is a necessary connection between the establishment of a free-market economy based on ordoliberal principles and the shape and extent of social policy in such a system. An agenda in support of a strong active social policy would have consequences for the economic policy of the respective state, since it would clearly require an interventionist approach, while ordoliberalism certainly is a non-interventionist economic philosophy.

Following the euro crisis and the policy of austerity which was imposed by EU institutions on EU member states such as Greece, Spain, Ireland, and Portugal as a means to address the crisis, there have been some studies that discussed ordoliberalism as ideational influence on the creation of the Economic and Monetary Union of the EU and on the measures of crisis mitigation taken to address the euro crisis (Bonefeld 2017a, Cardwell and Snaith 2018, Dullien and Guérot 2012, Fouskas 2018; Moszynski 2015, Nedergaard and Snaith 2015, Ryner 2015). These studies primarily focus on monetary policy,[3] a policy area that was of little significance when the Treaty of Rome was signed. It is quite surprising that there are only very few studies which investigate the ideational influence of ordoliberalism on other areas of social and economic integration. The number of studies that are interested in ordoliberalism as an influence on competition policy and so-

---

3 Some observers criticized the management to the euro crisis for using authoritarian means to impose a neoliberal agenda on the EU, an approach which they refer to as "authoritarian liberalism" or "authoritarian neoliberalism" (Bruff 2017, p. 151, Candeias, Oberndorfer, and Steckner 2014, p. 3, Sotiris 2017, p. 183, Somek 2015, pp. 73-74).

cial policy of the EU is rather limited. Akman and Kassim (2010, p. 126) list several studies which treat ordoliberalism as theoretical foundation of EU competition law and policy. However, most of these are not in-depth analyses of this specific issue. Nedergaard (2019, 2013) has deeply investigated the ideational influence of ordoliberalism on European integration in the areas of competition policy, agricultural policy, and monetary policy[4] and developed a methodological approach that allows to explore such influence on the integration process. This study strongly relies on Nedergaard's work. Joerges and Rödl (2004), Walters and Haahr (2005), and Young (2014) have analyzed the ordoliberal influence on social policy in the EU. Their insights are relied on in the chapter on social policy.

This study will, firstly, give an outline of ordoliberal theory and its central element, the order framework for the economy. Secondly, it briefly analyzes the ordoliberal approach to social justice and the welfare state. Thirdly, it explores how far ordoliberal principles were adopted, when the EEC was concluded. This chapter will especially reflect on the compromise between French dirigisme and German ordoliberalism that emerged after the Treaty of Rome was gradually enacted with the launch of the Single Market. Lastly, this study will reflect on the legacy which ordoliberalism left for European economic and social integration to date and briefly comment on the discussion about the ordoliberal influence on monetary integration of the EU.

4 Nedergaard also analyzed the ordoliberal influence on monetary policy. But this policy area will be excluded here, as has been explained above.

Basic Tenets of Ordoliberalism

Ordoliberalism is an economic theory which was developed in Germany at the end of the 1920s, beginning of the 1930s by scholars such as Walter Eucken, Franz Böhm, Wilhelm Röpcke, Alexander Rüstow, Leonhard Miksch, Alfred Müller-Armack and others. They are often referred to as the *Freiburg School*. This school of thought was very influential in the first years of German economic recovery after the Second World War. The *social market economy* which was established there was primarily based on ordoliberal principles, even though this does not mean that economic development in Germany at the time was purely ordoliberal. There were other influences such as Keynesianism and the Bismarckian welfare state which also left their mark on the post-war developments in Germany (Havertz 2019).

For ordoliberals the most important value is freedom. When they talk about freedom, they primarily mean the freedom of individuals to pursue their interests in the market, not so much civil liberties. "The fundamental question at the heart of ordoliberal thought is how to sustain market liberty." (Bonefeld 2012) Their concept of freedom is closely tied to that of competition. Freedom can only exist when the highest possible level of competition is secured for the economy. Walter Eucken (2004, p. 246), the central figure of the *Freiburg School*, envisioned "perfect competition" as the preferable status of power relations in the economy. Perfect competition can only be achieved if the concentration of economic power and thus the creation of monopolies and oligopolies is prevented. In the literature of early ordoliberals and in the writings of their followers, the approach to competition was further refined, and it was acknowledged that perfect competition was difficult to be achieved in reality. It must therefore be perceived as an ideal-type. The theoretical approach of perfect competition was then replaced by "workable competition," which is more pragmatic and considers the impact of economic power on "consumer choice" (Behrens 2014, p. 27). In this context, it is of interest that the European Commission (1966, p. 59) in its *Ninth General Report on the Activities of the Community* explicitly referred to workable competition when it named the establishment of an "effective and workable competitive system" as one of the main goals of European economic integration.

The ordoliberals concluded that securing the highest possible level of competition for the market would require a regulatory (that is, an institutional-legal) approach, involving a strong state that can establish and monitor a "framework order" for the economy based on which all participants act freely without direct government interference in the market (Eucken 2012a, p. 77). Government would only become active in case of a violation of the framework order. From an ordoliberal point of view, a sustainable economic order can only be established and maintained when the state gets involved in this process. This is where German ordoliberalism differs from Anglo-Saxon neoliberalism which trusts that an economic order will appear spontaneously when the forces of the market are allowed to play out non-interfered. In the decades before the First World War, the belief in laissez-faire capitalism was also prevalent in Germany. This changed after the war when a period began which Eucken described as a time of economic experimentation where the economic process and order was under the control of a state which actively regulated market activities. Economic freedom was even more restricted during the period of the Nazi regime which focused on the central control of the economic process (Eucken 2012b).

As Viktor Vanberg (2001, p. 2) noted, competition was held in very high esteem by the scholars of the *Freiburg School*:

> Competition means availability of alternative counterparts for trade, of alternative sources for supply, a condition that reduces the dependence of consumers on any particular supplier and, thereby, reduces the power that such dependence would provide to the latter.

To secure the highest possible level of competition, the concentration of economic power had to be prevented, even if it meant to tear up larger corporations in order to curtail their economic power (Eucken 2012c). The state had to step in and create the framework order for the economy and then pursue an order policy which would ensure that all actors played by the rules which were established with that order (*Ordo* is Latin for order.) What the ordoliberals had in mind was the establishment of a "competitive order" (Müller-Armack 1978, p. 327). Hence, the main focus of the framework order would be on securing competition.

For this theoretical approach to work in practice, the framework order would have to be complemented by an ethic that provides orientation not only for the individuals in their market activities but also in their social relations. Which means that ordoliberalism can be understood as "holistic conception of political economy that goes some way beyond the mere economics of the market" (Sally 1996, p. 234). The German social market economy, the political-economic system which emerged in Germany after the Second World War, was conceptualized not only as an economic but also as a social order (Müller-Armack 1978). The ordoliberal understanding of ethics has some resemblance with Immanuel Kant's ethic;[5] and Eucken's approach also has some religious implications (Wörsdörfer 2010). But it has to be noted that

---

5 Eucken's (1989, p. 35) critique of the combination of economic power with state power is clearly modeled on Kantian ethics where he claims that under these circumstances, "man becomes a tiny part in the anonymous, state-run economic machine," and the individual turns into an object and "loses his character as a person. The machine is an end in itself and man is the means by which the end is achieved."

this ethic was primarily meant to secure the long-term functioning of the market economy. It first and foremost was conceptualized as an entrepreneurial ethic. Eucken suggested that an educational effort was to be made so as to spread basic economic knowledge throughout society and instill an entrepreneurial attitude in all citizens (Ptak 2004). This entrepreneuralization would go hand in hand with the de-proletarianization of the German society (Röpcke 1962). Basically, ordoliberals envisioned the future of German society as one of entrepreneurs.

In this system, social policy was not seen as a means to directly improve the living conditions of German citizens. In the ordoliberal conception, social policy is understood as having an auxiliary function for the economy. Measures of social policy are expected to facilitate the smooth functioning of the free market. In the words of Werner Bonefeld (2017b, p. 6), "ordoliberal social policy intervenes in the 'human disposition' to enable a competitive order." Any active social policy not serving this purpose is plainly rejected.

Ordoliberal Influences on Competition Policy of the EEC

There are many indices that one of the main influences of ordoliberals on the Treaty of Rome was in the area of competition law. Most member countries of the EC did not have a competition law as elaborate as that of Germany when they joined the EEC. Their first experience with competition law was in the framework of the ECSC (Nedergaard 2019). It is widely acknowledged in the literature that German ordoliberals made a strong contribution to the shaping of the competition law of the EEC (Gerber 1998, Montalban, Ramirez-Perez, and Smith 2011, Nedergaard 2019, Walters and Haahr 2005). This view is supported by the fact that the first Commissioner for Competition of the EEC was Hans von der Groeben (1958-1970), who was mainly responsible for the order framework that was established for the EEC with the Treaty of Rome (Löffler 2003, p. 553):

> Especially, Hans von der Groeben personally left no doubt in his competition and order political orientation. The Spaak Report, for instance, named the expansion of European markets and competition as well as the elimination of the discrimination of any kind and the firm installation and monitoring of competition rules as core elements of the future EEC.

Von der Groeben had strong ties to the ordoliberal school of thought (Gerber 1998). He also was a co-author of the Spaak Report which was the draft treaty for the negotiations of the EEC and therefore strongly influenced the formation of the Community (Montalban, Ramirez-Perez, and Smith 2011). In this context it is interesting that Ernst Albrecht, a proponent of ordoliberalism and father of the new President of the European Commission Ursula von der Leyen from Germany, was the cabinet chief of von der Groeben in Brussels (1958-1969) and later took on the responsibility as head of the directorate general of the Commissioner for Competition (1969-1976) (Wigger 2008). Another personality of importance in this context is Alfred Müller-Armack, who was the German chief negotiator of the Treaty of Rome (Fouskas 2018). Müller-Armack (1947, p. 88) has coined the term "social market economy", which he envisioned as a "socially controlled market economy" and is one of the most important representatives of ordoliberalism in Germany. He naturally pursued an ordoliberal agenda when negotiating the treaty, even though it was not explicitly called that way. In fact, any explicit reference to the "social market economy" of Germany has deliberately been avoided, as Ludwig Erhard and Müller-Armack (1972, p. 349) explained in a manifesto supporting the idea of the social market economy:

> The treaty includes no explicit commitment to the social market economy. At the time when the Treaty of Rome was drafted it was too much of a German specialty, and the German negotiators also avoided it for reasons of international tact to characterize the Common Market explicitly as a variety of the social market economy.

In this context, it has to be noted that in the early years of the EEC, competition policy was not seen as an area of primary importance, and competition law was not vigorously enforced. This is due to the French influence which focused on the unrestricted creation of large corporations that were able to attain dominant positions in the newly created common market (Nedergaard, 2013). Competition policy only gained in importance with the implementation of the Single Market Program of the EU (Nedergaard 2019). Naturally, with the increasing importance of this policy field, the influence of ordoliberalism was more strongly felt in the EU. However, the fact that competition policy was not of eminent importance in the first years of European integration and that competition rules were not consequently enforced at the time does not mean that ordoliberalism did not have any influence on the treaty which laid the main foundations for the competition policy of the EU. It means that ordoliberal influence on policy implementation went through cycles with ups and downs in its implementation. But these fluctuations in implementation cannot serve to provide a basis for an argument against the assumption of an ideational influence of ordoliberalism right from the beginning of the European integration process, especially on the letter of the law of the treaty.

The Treaty of Rome was based on a compromise between few competing approaches. There was German ordoliberalism, and then there was French dirigisme, with ordoliberalism having the stronger and more lasting impact on the EC. Dirigisme relied heavily on Keynesianism and involved economic planning. After the Second World War, the French had instituted a national planning commission for their country which focused on indicative planning. The state took on the role as chief planner of the economy (Amable and Hanké 2001, p. 113). Which is why dirigisme can be seen as a statist approach. Dirigisme focused on the investment in specific regions and in the creation of "national champions" in the French economy. It was an approach that resulted in high levels of growth in the first one and a half decades after the war. When Charles de Gaulle became president of France in 1959, he embraced these statist policies and increased the involvement of the French government in dirigiste planning. This approach, of course, ran contrary to the principles of German ordoliberalism which wanted the state to largely stay out of economic affairs. While the French focused on a European planning project, the ordoliberals prioritized the creation of an "ordoliberal-inspired European Community based on competition policy" (Warlouzet 2019, p. 85). In his comparative analysis of dirigisme and ordoliberalism and their influence on European integration, Warlouzet (2019, p. 90) comes to the conclusion that neither completely dominated this process, while it has to be noted that ordoliberalism had a greater effect than dirigisme:

> German ordoliberalism has enjoyed greater influence, manifesting itself in implemented policies: competition policy and the EMU – and not only in projects, such as European planning. However, the influence of French dirigism has been visible first through the EEC/EU tolerance for national dirigism, and also through certain European policies, such

as support for R&D.

The EEC was based on neoliberal principles, especially on German ordoliberalism, which can be interpreted as a type of neoliberalism, differing from the (theoretical) pure form of the latter as advanced by scholars as Ludwig von Mises, Friedrich Hayek, and Milton Friedman primarily in its focus on the role of government in establishing and monitoring an order framework for the economy. At the center of ordoliberalism is an institutional-legal approach to competition. "Ordoliberal theory holds that public policy should be guided by the imperative of building a competitive market economy through upholding a set of credible rules and institutions." (Ban 2012, p. 138) From an ordoliberal point of view, what Europe needed was an "economic constitution" the core element of which would be the law regulating competition.

In the *Treaty Establishing the European Economic Community*, the centrality of competition law is highlighted in the preamble, which explains the principles of the treaty. Article 3 emphasizes the need to establish "a system that protects competition within the common market against distortions" (Treaty Establishing the EEC 1957, p. 15). Competition law was included in the treaty in articles 85-90. The most important regulations restricting the behavior of corporations which could undermine competition in the EC were incorporated in articles 85 and 86[6] (Treaty Establishing the EEC 1957). Article 85 prohibits all agreements of corporations or associations of firms that could affect trade among the member states and prevent, restrict, or distort competition within the common market. It explicitly prohibits price fixing, the restriction or control of production, supply, technical development or

6 Articles 101 and 102 of the *Consolidated Version of Treaty on the Functioning of the European Union.*

investments, the division of markets, discriminating treatment of business partners, and certain tying procedures (which tie specific conditions to contracts which have no relation to the subject of the contract). Article 86 primarily deals with the abuse of market power by corporations that have a dominant market position. Both articles explicitly mention consumer interests and the need to make competition policy in the interest of consumers. This may, as article 85 elaborates in paragraph 3, also involve exemptions from this law, if they are decided under the appropriate involvement of consumers and constitute an improvement in the production or distribution of commodities, or facilitate technological or economic progress.

Clearly, protecting and enabling consumer choice is at the heart of European competition law (Behrens 2014); and this focus on consumer choice is different from the classical liberal approach of "consumer welfare," which involves the notion that free markets generally result in elevated levels of welfare for all market participants. The focus of competition law on consumer interest and consumer choice is more in line with ordoliberalism, since "the consumer is a representative of common interest in the ordoliberal philosophy. It is the actor towards which all economic political decision-making should be directed" (Nedergaard 2013, p. 7). In his analysis of ordoliberalism and its operationalization in the competition policy of the EU Nedergaard (2019, p. 10) found that a rules-based system has been established which is now part of the "raison d'etre of EU competition policy;" the way principles of competition policy were established does have "the character of an economic constitution," and is thus very much in line with ordoliberal intentions; and a market was constructed which was "deliberately cultivated toward competition."

Another area of significance for competition policy regulated by the Treaty of Rome is state aid (articles 92-94[7]). Article 92 of the treaty says that state aid which distorts competition insofar as it impedes international trade is irreconcilable with the Common Market, especially when it provides certain corporations or industrial sectors advantages in this market (Treaty Establishing the EEC 1957). Nedergaard (2019) stressed that in the period running up to the creation of the Single Market, state aid was quite common and very popular in the member states of the EC. It has been reined in only with the creation of the Single Market; but reinforcement was again relaxed when the euro crisis struck and a temporary framework was introduced "allowing governments to grant loans and state guarantees and direct aid to banks and companies" (Nedergaard 2019, p. 13). As Nedergaard (2019, p. 12) noted, "mergers (Regulation No. 4046/89 and No. 139/2004) have also come under the regulative principles of EU competition policy." However, this happened many years after the Treaty of Rome came into force with the Merger Control Regulation of 1989 and later reforms, especially with the modernization of EU competition policy in 2004 (Nedergaard 2013). Since this study is focused on the Treaty of Rome, the regulation of mergers will not be treated in more depth here.

However, few scholars are doubtful about the influence of ordoliberalism on European economic integration. Pinar Akman (2012), for instance, argued that ordoliberalism cannot be a theoretical foundation of the EEC, because one of the main goals of the EEC is securing efficiency for the European market, while efficiency is not seen as a main objective of ordoliberal competition law. According to Behrens (2014, p. 27) this argument misinterprets the ordoliberal approach to efficiency:

---

7 Articles 106 to 108 of the *Consolidated Version of the Treaty on the Functioning of the European Union.*

> Ordoliberalism has always appreciated and emphasized the positive welfare (i.e. efficiency) effects of competition, but it refuses to measure the allocative or dynamic efficiency effects of individual business strategies which are instead left to pass the test of "consumers' choice" in the market.

Behrens (2014, p. 28) stresses that we would have to distinguish between different types of economic efficiency: "productive, allocative and dynamic efficiency." While it may be easy to measure the productive efficiency of a particular business strategy on the level of an individual firm, it will be almost impossible to measure allocative and dynamic efficiency (and changes in it) on the level of a whole society. "It follows that at least the determination of allocative and dynamic efficiency effects of a specific business strategy must be deferred to the competitive process that allows consumers to make their choices." Behrens (2014, p. 28) points to the efficiency defense of article 85 "for the justification of an anti-competitive agreement or concerted practice." Article 85 (3) allows for some exemptions from competition rules in cases where this increases efficiency in the production and distribution of goods and contributes to technical and economic progress; and it explicitly mentions the need for a participation of consumers in the decisions on these exemptions (Treaty Establishing the EEC 1957).

Angela Wigger (2017) put forward another argument against ordoliberal influence on the EEC. She even questioned the influence of ordoliberalism on the social market economy of Germany. She claimed that "the substantive content of EC/EU competition rules reflects, at best, a very much watered-down version of ordoliberal notions" (Wigger 2017, p. 163). Her main argument is that there would be no large-scale corporations in Europe anymore, had ordoliberal ideas been consequently adopted by European law and implemented by its competition policy. According to Wigger (2017, p. 175), it would be misleading to interpret article 86 (82 TEC, 102 TFEU) of the Treaty Establishing the EEC "as an anti-monopoly law with strong ordoliberal tenets," because the law did not prohibit a dominant market position, only the abuse of such a position. She also criticized that the provisions on competition in the Treaty of Rome were "formulated in vague and ambiguous terms" (Wigger 2008, p. 147) and that there were no merger control rules included in the treaty. This critique neglects that ordoliberal thought has developed and matured over time. Wigger's critique would have some merit, if one expected that original ordoliberal ideas were adopted par for par in their pure form, that is, as the ideal-type with a focus on "perfect competition." But as already pointed out earlier, ordoliberal theory has advanced over time and become more pragmatic. Ordoliberals came to accept "workable competition," as type of competition that could actually be achieved in the real world (Behrens 2014, p. 27). They had to acknowledge that competition will inevitably result in differences in economic power and concluded that it was necessary to prevent the abuse of that power, not the accumulation of economic power per se.

The Ordoliberal Approach to Social Justice and Its Influence on the EEC

The Treaty of Rome includes a larger section on social policy in Title III, articles 117 to 128. In article 117 (1), it says that the member states agree about the necessity to improve the living and working conditions of the labor force and stresses the need for a harmonization of these conditions in the EC. In article 117 (2), it states that these desirable developments could be best achieved through the formation of the common market as prescribed by the treaty. Article 118 talks about the "close collaboration" of the member states on the main issue areas of social policy such as employment, occupational education, social security and labor standards at the work place (Treaty Establishing the EEC 1957, pp. 61-62). This means that the member states trust that economic integration will result in these desirable social outcomes and that social policy primarily remains in the authority of the individual member states.

This approach appears to be in keeping with the basic tenets of ordoliberalism on social justice. Ordoliberals were certainly interested in questions of social justice. They assumed that social justice could be achieved in a system where the government imposes a regulatory framework for economic activity but does not interfere in the market, assuming that a well-functioning free market will secure social justice, because in such a system everyone would be rewarded according to their merits, that is, their abilities, endeavor, and ingenuity. Ideally, individuals would be conscious of their moral responsibility and act accordingly when they pursue their interests in the market. In their conception of social justice, ordoliberals focus on the personal responsibility of the individual and connect it with the merit principle that rewards them according to their achievements (Hecker 2014). Which means that ordoliberals are interested in the just outcome of economic activities. This is an approach to social justice which sets them apart from laissez-faire liberals, who principally have no such interest. This was acknowledged by Willgeroth and Peacock (1989, p. 6) who noted that ordoliberals "in contrast to laissez-faire-liberals" are "confirmed end-state liberals." For laissez-faire liberals, distribution is a matter of individual choice. An individual participates in the distribution of resources in a specific manner, because she chooses to do so, or as Robert Nozick

(1974, p. 160) famously phrased: "*From each as they choose, to each as they are chosen.*"[8] The focus of ordoliberalism on the merit principle means that it does more than just accept social inequality, when practically applied in the real world, it consciously produces inequality; where competition is the guiding principle, there will be winners and losers. The economic and social differences which increasingly divide Germany (Spannagel 2018), where ordoliberal principles have been applied in economic policy for decades, are a result of this process.

From an ordoliberal point of view, social inequality is a necessary element of a just society. Differences in ability and effort will naturally result in differences in outcome. The emphasis on the merit principle just means that the distribution of resources has to conform to some standard of fairness, where the outcome which an individual achieves is related to the performance of that individual. For ordoliberals this is a question of performance-related justice (Leistungsgerechtigkeit). Müller-Armack (1981, p. 92) reduced this principle of justice to a simple formula:

> Who is committed to freedom as a moral value, to real competition of performance and to free pricing as an organizing principle of the economy, understands social justice not as 'the same to everyone' but as 'to each his own,' on account of his achievements.

Where this principle rules there is no need for a comprehensive social policy. In fact, ordoliberals just as their Anglo-Saxon neoliberal counterparts abhor the social welfare state (Ptak 2016). From an ordoliberal point of view, the welfare state undermines the sense of responsibility that can be expected from an individual who is active in the market for her own well-being. According

8 Emphasis in the original.

to Hamm (1989), it potentially brings about an attitude that is detrimental to the goals of economic growth and the increase of productivity, and it is counterproductive to the intended entrepreneuralization of the citizens in a country with a free-market economy.

For ordoliberals, social policy can be neglected because the framework order for the economy which is at the center of ordoliberal thinking, will provide for a society that has little need for any redistributive measures. They trust that a well-ordered economy will result in a high level of productivity in which all members of society can participate and get their fair share according to their efforts and abilities. "It seems that ordoliberals regarded social policy as an inherent aspect of *Ordnungspolitik*, implying that a well-functioning competitive market would not need a social policy." (Young 2014, pp. 283-284) Therefore, they saw no need to include comprehensive articles of social policy in the Treaty of Rome and assumed that the establishment of a framework order on European level would suffice to guarantee a socially desirable outcome of market activities. When the Treaty of Rome was concluded, "a European 'social model' was not on the agenda. More positively speaking: The 'social' remained in the political sphere – and hence a matter of national concern" (Joerges and Rödl 2004, p. 4).

Walters and Haahr (2005, p. 51), agreed that the EC "lacked extensive powers and competences within the social field." But they stressed that the few provisions on social policy that were included in the Treaty of Rome in articles 117-128 are designed "in ways that are to supplement and promote the workings of the common market" (ibid.). They, for instance, point to the creation of the European Social Fund (articles 123-127), the purpose of which was to "increase the 'geographical and occupational mobility' of workers within the Community, thereby contributing to improvements in the overall employment situation and standards of living." They conclude that the provisions on social policy included in the treaty primarily serve "economic rationalization" which they interpret as "quite consistent with ordoliberal principles" (ibid.).

From an ordoliberal point of view, in a society with a competitive order there is no need for an extensive social welfare state, especially if society is ordered in a way which ensures that those who lose out in the competitive game fall softly and are caught in a network of strong social institutions which help them getting back on their feet. This requires the inclusion of all citizens in social institutions such as family, neighborhood, and church communities (Hecker 2011). This is where the social-conservative implications of ordoliberalism become evident, and where ordoliberalism reveals its character as a right-liberal economic philosophy. This is one reason why ordoliberalism is attracting the New Right in Germany who combine it with ethnic nationalism (Havertz 2019).

To conclude, the author agrees with Walters and Haahr (2005) that the provisions on social policy in the treaty on the EEC are consistent with ordoliberalism. They primarily serve economic rationalization and do not impose any larger commitment to an extensive social policy or an active welfare state on the member states. Instead, they leave the decision on the extent and direction of social policy largely at the discretion of the individual member states. In applying Nedergaard's (2013) methodological approach which suggests to distinguish between potential alternatives to ordoliberalism as an ideational source for the social policy of the EC, one would have to think about how far the social policy as agreed in the Treaty of Rome conforms to laissez-faire liberalism and dirigisme or Keynesianism, respectively. Here we face the difficulty that the approach of ordoliberalism and laissez-faire liberalism in their principal rejection of an active welfare state cannot be distinguished accurately. However, it could be said that social policy as included in the Treaty of Rome conforms more to ordoliberalism than laissez-faire liberalism, because the provisions in articles 117-128 can be seen as function of the economy and as such – in a broader sense – be seen as an element of the economic constitution that was set up with the treaty. The insignificant role for social policy in the Treaty is certainly in contrast to dirigisme and to any other type of Keynesianism. Hence, they can clearly be excluded as ideational source for these provisions of the treaty.

Conclusion

Ordoliberal notions have been very influential in the formation of the EEC, especially for its competition law. The impact of ordoliberal ideas can still be felt today in the contemporary competition policy of the EU. However, just as ordoliberal ideas were not realized in their pure form in Germany, this is also true for economic integration in the European Community. According to Nedergaard (2013, p. 15), the influence of ordoliberalism fluctuated over time and "the unfolding of market forces as part of the EU's competition policy has for long periods definitely been very different from both laissez-faire liberalism and ordoliberalism." French dirigisme clearly had a strong influence on the lax implementation of competition law before the implementation of the Single Market Program. The Treaty of Rome is not a genuinely ordoliberal document; neither was the process of economic integration that followed on the signing of that treaty solely influenced by ordoliberalism. It was based on a compromise between two competing approaches: French dirigisme and German ordoliberalism, with the latter making its influence more strongly felt than the former (Warlouzet 2019). The fact that there were many ideological influences on the Treaty of Rome resulted in accounts which either downplay the effect of ordoliberalism on this agreement (Akman and Kassim 2010) or reject the idea of any larger effect of ordoliberalism on it (Wigger 2017). By contrast, this paper holds that European integration cannot be properly understood without the acknowledgement of the ordoliberal influence on its economic and social dimension. It is an influence the strength of which varied over time and which can still be felt today.

An important outcome of the efforts of ordoliberals was the almost complete exclusion of social policy from the Treaty of Rome. Even though there were few provisions on social policy, it is noteworthy that the scope of social policy was rather limited. The founders of the EEC agreed to avoid any more comprehensive commitment of the EC and leave responsibility of social policy largely to the individual member states. The low salience which social policy has today in the framework of the EU can be seen as a legacy of the early ideational influence of ordoliberalism on the process of both economic and social integration. It could be shown that both are interconnected and that social policy can primarily be seen as an auxiliary policy for the smooth functioning of the free-market economy in Europe.

Future research could look deeper into the mandates which were given to the delegations of Germany and France for the negotiation of the Treaty of Rome and gain deeper insights on the competing influence of ordoliberalism and dirigisme on that treaty.

Chapter 4

The Single European Act

New Impetus for the Internal Market

Introduction

There had been a lull in the process of European integration in the period from the middle of the 1960s to the beginning of the 1980s. The "Empty Chair Crisis" of 1965-1966 had already brought a stalemate in this process; and it was prolonged through the economic crises that occurred during the 1970s, especially with the oil crises of 1973 and 1980. The terms "Europessimism" and "Eurosclerosis" made the rounds (Zimmermann and Dür 2016; Holmes 1991, p. 30; Moravcsik 1991, p. 19). The Single European Act (SEA) was meant to revitalize this process. The treaty was signed in February 1986 and came into force on July 1, 1987. It comprised a number of institutional reforms, some of which involved the change of the voting procedure in the Council of Ministers from unanimity to qualified majority voting (QMV). This reform was meant to ease and speed up the decision-making process in the Council. Another major institutional reform concerned the European Parliament which was given greater powers with the introduction of the cooperation procedure. Article 6 (4) of the

SEA amends the Treaty establishing the European Economic Community of 1957, where it revises the original provision with the following phrase: "[…] the Council shall, acting on a proposal from the Commission, in cooperation with the European Parliament and after consulting the Economic and Social Committee." The crucial innovation in this passage is the phrase "in cooperation with the European Parliament." In the years following the coming into force of the SEA, the cooperation procedure was used frequently in decisions that spurred up the formation of the Single European Market (SEM) (Craig and de Búrca 2003). The third major institutional reform brought about by the SEA was the legal recognition of the European Council, which was for the first time included in one of the European treaties (Berman 1989).

The treaty's purpose was primarily to facilitate the completion of the single market and reanimate the European integration process. In Article 8a, the treaty defined a period during which all the measures were to be implemented that aimed at creating an internal market "the free movement of goods, persons, services and capital" (Single European Act 1987, p. 7). The treaty stated that this process should be completed by December 31, 1992. The SEM was indeed implemented on January 1, 1993. Since then, European economic integration in the SEM contributed to economic growth in several areas, including GDP, jobs, intra-EU trade and the share of exports in the composition of the individual member states' economic output (Thirion 2017). Despite these positive outcomes, there are still areas where the SEM has not been fully realized. According to Marek Dabrowski (2023), this concerns all the four main freedoms which the SEM was supposed to establish evenly throughout the bloc.

This chapter analyzes the measures which the SEA prescribed in order to move the EU closer to achieving its goal of establishing a fully-fledged common market without significant obstacles to the free flow of goods, persons, services and capital. How far could the single market provisions of the SEA be fully implemented, and what are the circumstances and the inhibiting factors that led to restrictions of those freedoms? This study looks at the obstacles that still existed for the implementation of some of the measures which the EU tried to achieve with the launch of the SEM. There are signs that the market was never fully completed, and there is also reason to assume that reversals could happen where a high level of integration has already been reached (Dabrowski 2023).

The European Community had early on adopted the goal of creating a single market with the Treaty of Rome, which was signed in 1957 and came into force in 1958. It launched the European Economic Community (EEC) which had the explicit purpose of establishing a common market. The signatories of the treaty, the six original member states, assumed that a transition period of twelve years would eventually lead to the creation of this common market (Treaty establishing the European Economic Community [EEC], 2015). One of the cornerstones of this process was the formation of a customs union. The customs union came into being in 1968 (European Union n.d.). It had wider implications for the liberalization of trade within the Community, since it involved the establishment of a free trade area. It also included the adoption of a common external tariff (CET) and resulted in the need for a common external trade policy.

As Brian T. Hanson (1998, p. 68, cf. 48) noted, even though tariff barriers for trade had been removed with this customs union, "individual countries retained control over a myriad of nontariff barriers, which they imposed more or less at will." There were a number of other factors that slowed down the integration process, chief of which was the mixed results of the Community's attempt to harmonize trade-related standards and regulations throughout the community. When Jacques Delors became the president of the European Commission in 1984 the mood was not very good in the European Community. According to Peter Holmes (1991, p. 30), "The proliferation of national trade policy measures risked undermining the established gains from economic integration and threatened to block all progress towards full economic union."

It was the British member of the Delors Commission, Arthur Cockfield, who in 1985 took the initiative to give a decisive boost to the formation of the common market. He wrote a white paper for the European Commission with 300 recommendations for an improvement of the internal operations of this market. (The number of these recommendations was later reduced to 279.) Cockfield argued for the complete removal of physical border controls which were still in place at the time: "The reason for getting rid entirely of physical and other controls between Member States is not one of theology or appearance, but the hard practical fact that the maintenance of any internal frontier controls will perpetuate the costs and disadvantages of a divided market." (European Commission 1985, p. 126) The Commission also asserted that further action was necessary beyond the mere removal of border controls and addressed the need for the removal of non-tariff barriers, particularly technical barriers to trade: "It is through the elimination of technical barriers that the Community will give the large market its economic and industrial dimension by enabling industries to make economies of scale and therefore to become more competitive." (ibid.)

Many of Cockfield's recommendations were later included in the SEA. His white paper distinguished between three different kinds of barriers: physical, technical and fiscal barriers. With its recommendation for 279 new directives the white paper focused on the removal of these barriers (Holmes 1991). The treaty comprises a wide range of measures on the economic and monetary integration of the Community that were meant to amend the EEC treaty in a way that would enable the Community to achieve the establishment of the internal market by the time limit which the SEA set for the end of 1992.

Significant Provisions on Economic Integration

To facilitate the completion of the SEM, the SEA amended the Treaty establishing the European Economic Community in several ways. Some of the articles of the EEC treaty were supplemented, others were partly or wholly replaced by the new provisions included in the SEA. This primarily concerned articles 8, 28, 57, 59, 70, 84, 99, and 100. Whereas articles 8 and 100 were supplemented by new provisions that were added to the existing ones, articles 28, 57, 59, 70, and 99 were entirely or partly replaced. Article 84 was partly replaced and also supplemented.

In the following this chapter will examine the specific changes that were made to each of these articles of the EEC treaty and point out the specific meaning which they had for the economic integration of the Community. Article 13 of the SEA stipulates the supplementation of Article 8 of the EEC treaty with Article 8a. The complicated timeframe for the integration process included in Article 8 was complemented by a more rigid and ambitious one in Article 8a, which stated that the single market was supposed to be fully established by December 31, 1992. Article 8a says that "the internal market shall comprise an area without internal frontiers" (Single European Act 1987, p. 8). Thus, it acknowledged that these frontiers still existed in February 1986 when the SEA was signed, despite the language in Article 8 of the EEC treaty which indicated the expectation that the process of economic integration would move forward at a faster pace than it actually did. The newly introduced Article 8a went beyond Article 8 in that it made the goal of establishing a unified internal market official (Holmes 1991). This involved a significant change to the treaty, since the objective of a completely integrated internal market had so far not been a clear priority of the Community. It endowed the European Commission with the requisite authority to decisively move forward with the process of economic integration. As Peter Holmes (1991, p. 30) put it, with this decisiveness the SEA symbolized "a renewed political willingness to allow the provisions of the Treaty of Rome to be implemented in full."

The SEA made several key institutional changes to the Treaty establishing the European Economic Community. These changes primarily focused on the decision-making processes within the European Community, particularly in relation to the creation of the SEM. One of the most important developments brought about by the SEA was the replacement of the requirement of unanimity for the decision-making within the Council of Ministers by QMV. This affected the decisions in a number of key areas related to the SEM. It is not by accident that the "provisions for qualified majority voting are mainly to be found in the section of the SEA dealing with the internal market," as David Allen (1992, p. 35) observed. There is a number of articles in this section of the treaty that were all "amended to replace unanimity with qualified majority voting" (ibid.). This includes articles 8a, 8b, 8c, 28, 57 (2), 59, 70 (1) and 84. In addition, the SEA introduced article 100a, which can be seen as the cornerstone in the Commission's attempt to make the decisions on harmonization in the Council of Ministers easier by the introduction of QMV.

Most EU scholars see article 100a as the core innovation of the SEA. It provided the Council with the opportunity to use QMV for many matters concerning the creation of the single market. This change was implemented because the previous requirement of unanimity for decisions in the Council hampered the decision-making process in this governmental body of the Community severely: "Application of the unanimity requirement allowed a dissenting Member State to block legislation indefinitely until substantial compromises favoring its position were made." (Potter 1993, p. 257) According to Barbara C. Potter (ibid.) this essentially endowed individual member states with the power to veto any decision which they viewed as opposed to their national interest.

The Empty Chair Crisis occurred in 1965-1966, when French President Charles de Gaulle decided that it was time to boycott the Council of Ministers. The French did not participate in meetings of the Council, which back then was the most important decision-making body of the European Communities. They left their seat at the table of the council empty (hence, the phrase Empty Chair Crisis). With this tactic de Gaulle challenged the supranational decision-making power of the Commission. It was a reaction to proposals by Walter Hallstein, the president of the European Commission, to increase the powers of the Commission and make it more independent by giving it its "own resources" through the introduction of agricultural levies and customs duties that would directly go to the European Community (Caraffini 2015).

This crisis was resolved by the Luxembourg Compromise of 1966, which was "an informal agreement that required unanimity on all questions a member deemed important" concerning its national interests (Keohane and Hoffman 1991, p. 7). Based on this agreement each member state could claim the need for unanimity in decision-making whenever they considered decisions made by the Community as detrimental to their particular interests. It essentially gave them veto power. In this situation the Community lived "with the sword of Damocles" over its head, since it was always possible that a member state might "invoke its national vital interest and practice a new empty chair policy in order to avoid being put in a minority" (Grin 2020, 158). This is the main reason why the Luxembourg Compromise ushered in a period of stagnation in the process of economic integration of the Community.

According to Laurent Warlouzet (2020), the SEA annulled the Luxembourg Compromise and replaced it with the provisions in article 100a which expanded QMV to many areas of Community decision-making. Potter (1993, p. 260) noted that "any discussion of it [the Luxembourg Compromise, R. H.] is conspicuously absent in the SEA." However, according to Potter (ibid.), paragraphs 4 and 5 of article 100a are still in the spirit of the Luxembourg Compromise. She referred to these sections as an "approximate codification of this gentlemen's agreement" (ibid.). Article 100a (5) includes a safeguard measure which authorizes individual member states to take protective actions in internal trade in form of quantitative restrictions in case one of the harmonization measures instituted by the SEA affects any of the areas mentioned in article 36 of the EEC treaty (SEA 1987). Article 36 states that such action would be justified

> on grounds of public morality, public order, public safety, the protection of human or animal life or health, the preservation of plant life, the protection of national treasures of artistic, historical or archaeological value or the protection of industrial and commercial property. (Treaty establishing the European Economic Community 2015)

George A. Berman (1989, p. 543) described the provisions included in Article 100a (5) as "fairly traditional mechanism" as they allowed an individual member state to protect its vital interests in keeping with article 36 of the EEC treaty. Article 100a

(4) has caused far more controversy (Berman 1989). Under article 100a (4), member states had been granted a possible exemption from implementing decisions that were made based on a qualified majority vote. In order to make use of such exemptions, it was decided that member states would have to notify the Commission that "major needs" of this member state were affected by the measure concerned. The Commission would then have had to verify that any disparate national laws that were implemented by a member state in derogation of the harmonization measures that it deviated from were "not a means of arbitrary discrimination or a disguised restriction on trade between Member States" (SEA 187, p. 8). The inclusion of article 100a (4) in the SEA resulted in concerns that "the member states may rely too heavily on the safeguard provisions of the Single Act and thereby circumvent the implementation of Council decisions taken by qualified majority vote" (Good 1988, p. 320). However, these concerns turned out to be overstated, since there has not been any excessive abuse of these provisions.

The inclusion of these articles resulted in an increase of QMV in the Council and thus enabled this institution "to pass legislation more easily over the objection of minority states" (Berman 1989, p. 583) According to a report of the European Commission (as cited in Keohane and Hoffmann 1991, p. 7) from 1988, "the now fully accepted possibility of adopting a decision by a qualified majority forces the delegations to display flexibility throughout the debate, thus making decisionmaking easier." With QMV, governments may occasionally be forced to accept significant deviations from their national policy stances and regulatory traditions in order to implement a decision made based on QMV (Micossi 2016). At the same time, it may make a government more inclined to accept or enter into a compromise within the Council (ibid.). This is certainly the impact which it had on the decisions that were made on the implementation of the internal market. The use of QMV for the harmonization of national policies concerning the internal market facilitated the process of economic integration and allowed for the completion of the SEM in its preliminary version by the targeted date of December 31, 1992.

What is also remarkable about the SEA is a change of language in Article 100a (1), where it talks about "measures" which the Council shall adopt "for the approximation of the provisions laid down by law, regulation or administrative action in Member States which have as their object the establishment and functioning of the internal market" (SEA 1987, p. 8). As Potter (1993, p. 258) noted, "this language is far broader than that, of article 100 itself, which requires the Council to adopt 'directives.'" This change had far-reaching consequences, since it significantly increased the number of legislative instruments which the Council could use in its effort to harmonize rules throughout the whole of the Community. This was to a large part owed to the new approach which the Community took to the process of integration when it focused more on the mutual recognition of national standards and rules rather than their strict harmonization (ibid., p. 259). "Mutual recognition alleviates the severe political and logistical problems of harmonization and calls on Member States to recognize each other's national standards, assuming some acceptable threshold is met." (ibid.)

The adoption of QMV for many decisions concerning the economic integration of the European Community through the provisions in the SEA – especially in article 100a – advanced the harmonization of national laws throughout the Community. The promotion of the mutual recognition of standards was the second important instrument in the toolbox of the Commission which it used to facilitate this process. Mutual recognition asks member states to recognize each other's national standards if a certain level is attained that all parties find acceptable, and thus helps to avoid the serious political and practical issues associated with harmonization (ibid.).

For this purpose, the Commission relied on the case law of the European Court of Justice (ECJ), particularly the *Cassis de Dijon* case (Holmes 1991). This case from 1978 involved the German supermarket chain Rewe which was held by Rewe-Zentral AG, a retail corporation with headquarters in the West German city of Cologne. Rewe had imported the liquor Cassis de Dijon from France, which contained between 15 percent and 20 percent alcohol. However, the German agency responsible for the regulation of spirits, the Federal Monopoly Administration for Spirits (Bundesmonopolverwaltung für Branntwein), prohibited this import on the grounds that German law prescribed that spirits would at least have to have a content of 32 percent alcohol. After running its course through the German court system, the case was finally referred to the ECJ which in 1979 sided with Rewe and decided as follows:

> There is therefore no valid reason why, provided that they have been lawfully produced and marketed in one of the Member States, alcoholic beverages should not be introduced into any other Member State; the sale of such products may not be subject to a legal prohibition on the marketing of beverages with an alcohol content lower than the limit set by the national rules. (ECJ 1979, p. 664)

This landmark ruling by the court laid the foundation for the mutual recognition of standards in many areas involving cross-border trade among the member states of the Community. Stefano Micossi (2016, p. 9) emphasized the importance which this ruling had for the process of economic integration: "With one stroke a myriad of technical barriers to free movement of goods were made illegal, thus relieving the European Commission of the task of seeking new legislation to bring them down." Another important case that played a key role in bringing down non-tariff barriers to trade was the *Dassonville* case from 1974. Here the ECJ had decided that "all trading rules enacted by Member States which are capable of hindering, directly or indirectly, actually or potentially, intra-Community trade are to be considered as measures having an effect equivalent to quantitative restrictions" (ECJ 1974, p. 852). Such rules, the court concluded, were therefore inadmissible.

The application of mutual recognition had its limits when it came to certain issues which still required a binding regulatory approach. These issues included public "health standards," "additives," "labelling," as well as "official inspections designed to ensure that manufacturers comply with rules relating to health and safety protection" (Swann 1992, pp. 48-49). There were other restrictions to the purview of the SEA. There were several fields that were intentionally excluded from the scope of article 100a. This concerned "fiscal matters, the free movement of persons, and the treatment of employees" (Potter 1993, p. 259). Decisions on these issues still required unanimity when put to a vote in the Council of Ministers (ibid.).

These restrictions can largely be seen as the result of British attempts to limit the use of QMV as much as possible. According to Allen (1992, p. 35), the British government ensured that unanimity remained required for a larger number of issues such as "the harmonization of VAT rates, excise duties and other forms of indirect taxation—all matters of political sensitivity to Britain." These restrictions resulted in a great deal of disappointment in the countries that had originally founded the European Communities, since they would have preferred a much broader use of QMV (ibid.). Ultimately, the SEA was based on a compromise among countries that had different ideas about the pace and the scope of economic integration in Europe.

Conclusion

From the middle of the 1960s until the beginning of the 1980s, there was a slowdown in European integration, which was made worse by the Empty Chair Crisis and other economic difficulties like the oil crisis. Signed in 1986 and going into effect in 1987, the SEA introduced several institutional reforms to breathe new life into integration. This treaty was of crucial importance in preparing for the deeper economic integration of the European Community, the internal market in particular, and was at the same time indispensable as a legal gateway of the Community towards the creation of the European Union. In order to expedite the SEM's completion, the SEA modified the Treaty establishing the EEC. It involved a number of noteworthy amendments, such as the addition and removal of several articles, chief among them the new Article 8a, which established a December 31, 1992 deadline for the creation of the internal market. In many SEM-related sectors, the SEA replaced unanimity for decision-making within the Council of Ministers with QMV, easing the way for economic integration in the process.

The SEA promoted the mutual recognition of national standards to avoid the need for the harmonization of national laws in some sectors and relied on key rulings of the ECJ to remove non-tariff barriers to trade. Nonetheless, several areas such as budgetary concerns and the free movement of persons were not covered by QMV. The SEA can be characterized as an agreement that was reached by member states with varying perspectives regarding the pace and scope of the integration process.

Chapter 5

Maastricht and the Prospects of Fiscal Integration in the European Union

Introduction

The creation of the European monetary union with the Maastricht Treaty of 1992, which also established the European Union (EU), was a decisive step toward further economic integration of Europe and involved the acknowledgement that economic integration of a region needs to be complemented by monetary integration once this process has reached a certain stage. Hence, it was decided in Maastricht that the individual member states would give up their national currencies and replace them with a new European currency, the euro. The treaty also included a provision for the establishment of a central bank, the European Central Bank (ECB), which was to be tasked with implementing and overseeing European monetary policy.

When the euro zone was created, the member countries gave up their individual competences in the field of monetary policy. They lost the ability to react to external economic shocks with the devaluation of their currency – a measure which had been the standard reaction to such shocks when the individual member states still had the competence to pursue such policies. Devaluation was meant to restore competitiveness in international trade. With this default option lost, the only way to react to crises was for governments in the countries affected to work toward a decrease of wages and prices, and to cut spending. In the euro crisis, this organizational framework of the monetary union turned out to be detrimental to the quick recovery of the countries that were most strongly impacted by this crisis.

It will be shown in this study that it was the *design flaws* of the monetary union which primarily caused the protracted misery of the countries at the center of the euro crisis. This especially concerns Greece, the economy of which suffered immensely and whose social welfare state deteriorated due to the measures imposed on the country by the European institutions which managed the crisis and the International Monetary Fund (IMF) (Havertz 2014). The main hypothesis advanced in this paper is that it was the focus on the strict separation of monetary policy and fiscal policy which is at the root of the problems that emerged in the Economic and Monetary Union (EMU) of the EU with the euro crisis. When the 12 heads of state and government of the EU member states came together in Maastricht and decided about the introduction of a common currency, they made sure that this step of economic integration was strictly confined to monetary policy only and that integration in the field of fiscal policy was left out as far as possible. Those who were in favor of a *stability union* prevailed in the negotiations of the Maastricht Treaty (Hacker and Koch 2017). They were concerned that any type of fiscal integration could jeopardize the economic stability of the union, because it would create incentives for those not committed to stability to pursue an irresponsible fiscal policy at the expense of other member states who were committed to stability. It was the insistence on the systemic insolation of monetary policy from fiscal policy which partly caused and later exacerbated the euro crisis.

In the aftermath of the euro crisis, calls for further fiscal integration of the EU have become louder. Some observers have recognized that the only way forward toward deeper integration is through fiscal integration. This has been acknowledged by the Juncker commission as evidenced in the release of position papers by the commission that support further integration in this field (European Commission 2017; European Commission 2018). The coronavirus crisis, which was a health crisis and an economic crisis at the same time, and the reaction of the European Commission to this crisis under the leadership of Commission president Ursula von der Leyen has shown that deeper fiscal integration is possible, when they decided about an additional relief budget which involved considerably more spending and redistribution on community level than ever seen before in the EU (European Council 2020; European Commission 2020). This response to the crisis has shown that further integration in this field is possible and indeed necessary, if the European project of an "ever closer union" is supposed to become reality.

This study will in the second section give a brief overview of the historical developments of European monetary integration with a focus on the Maastricht Treaty and the creation of the euro. It will be shown why and how monetary policy was separated from fiscal policy when the monetary union was created. These considerations will also reflect on the theory of Optimal Currency Area (OCA) which is the leading theory on monetary union. The critique of this theory will focus on the lack of its attention to fiscal policy and the relation that necessarily exists between fiscal policy and monetary policy. The third section argues for the need of further integration of monetary and fiscal policy in the EU. It discusses the impact which the strict separation of these policies had during the euro crisis and analyzes the ideological obstacles to deeper integration in this field. The fourth section looks into proposals for future developments of fiscal policy in the EU and reflects on whether an independent fiscal policy on union level is a possible scenario for the future of the EU. This would be a necessary step in the process of European integration if the member countries of the EU ever plan to reach the highest stage of regional integration that is aimed at the creation of a political union. The fifth section gives an overview of the spending measures that were decided by the EU as a reaction to the coronavirus crisis which resulted in a remarkable increase of EU expenditures. In the past, the potential costs of a common fiscal policy have certainly contributed to the reluctance to take further steps in this policy field. However, the crisis has shown that higher levels of spending and the transfer of considerable sums from national to the European level are possible if the circumstances demand it. The question is whether the spending on such a high level can be maintained and if the transfers can somehow be replaced by the raising of the respective revenue on EU level. The article concludes with considerations about the potentials and limitations of fiscal policy in the EU in the medium- and long-term future.

A Brief History of the Economic and Monetary Union (EMU)

The process of European integration has continuously progressed and deepened since the first steps were made with the foundation of the European Coal and Steel Community (ECSC) in 1952 and the European Economic Community (EEC) in 1958. However, these first steps were primarily focused on the removal of barriers to trade and on the creation of a customs union which was successfully established by the six founding members of the European Communities (EC) in 1968. Initially, monetary policy was not high on the agenda of the EC.

The first move to some coordination of monetary policy was made with article 105 of the Treaty of Rome in 1957 which introduced a Monetary Advisory Committee. This committee had consultative status and was tasked with monitoring "the monetary and financial situation of the Member States and the Community as well as the general payment transactions of the Member States and to report regularly to the Council and the Commission" (Treaty Establishing the European Economic Community, 1957, p. 55). In article 104 the treaty formulates as an important goal of the EEC for all member states to have an even balance of payments in order to foster the stabilization of price levels and ensure trust in the currencies of all members states (Treaty Establishing the European Economic Community, 1957).

The next important step toward monetary integration was made with the Werner Report of 1970, which was named after the prime minister of Luxembourg, Pierre Werner, who drafted the report. It included a plan to introduce a common currency for all member states within ten years. The Werner Report (1970, p. 9) was concerned about a "structural and regional disequilibrium" that could be caused by the free movement of goods and services, people, and capital when the common market was fully implemented. The establishment of a single currency was seen as a counterweight against the emergence of such disequilibria. The report suggested that there were two ways to achieve that goal either by maintaining the individual currencies and putting them under centralized control or by the introduction of a single currency. The maintenance of individual currencies would nonetheless have meant full monetary integration, because it would have involved "the total and irreversible convertibility of currencies, the elimination of margins of fluctuation in rates of exchange, the irrevocable fixing of parity ratios and the total liberation of movements of capital" (Werner Report 1970, p. 26). Hence, had national monetary symbols been maintained, it would have been in name only. The report explicitly stated that the launch of a single currency was preferable to that second option, because "considerations of a psychological and political order militate in favour of the adoption of a single currency which would guarantee the irreversibility of the undertaking" (Werner Report 1970, p. 26). The report proposed a phased implementation of the monetary union in different stages. However, the oil crises of the 1970s and the breakdown of the Bretton Woods monetary system interfered with the project and delayed it considerably.

The plan proposed by Werner was never fully implemented. But there have been elements of the report which have been realized. This, for instance, concerns the "snake agreement" of 1972 which fixed the margins within which the exchange rates of the currencies of the member states were allowed to fluctuate at 2.25 percent (Myrus 1994). The snake agreement can be seen as "the Community's first coordinated effort to establish an exchange-rate mechanism" (Myrus 1994, p. 2109). It is interesting in the context of this study to note that the Werner Report (1970) included some provisions concerning the coordination and harmonization of the "budget policy" and "fiscal policy" of the individual member states. But that did nowhere in this document amount to considerations of a common fiscal policy.

The process of monetary integration took a new direction when the European Monetary System (EMS) was founded in 1979. The launch of the EMS was the result of a Franco-German initiative promoted by Valéry Giscard d'Estaing, the president of France, and German Chancellor Helmut Schmidt. The main aim of the EMS was to "reduce the disruptive impact of sizeable exchange rate devaluations and regulate changes in parities" (Mongelli 2008, p. 11). It included the introduction of the European currency unit (ECU) which was defined as a "basket of currencies" and an Exchange Rate Mechanism (ERM) which allowed variable exchange rates for the currencies of the member states but limited the fluctuation of bilateral exchange rates through the establishment of margins which were again set at 2.25 percent (Mongelli 2008).

In 1988, Jacques Delors, then president of the European Commission, had set up a committee that was tasked with exploring the feasibility of an economic and monetary union. It resulted in the Delors Report which outlined the establishment of the monetary union in three stages. Therefore, the Delors Report which was submitted to the European Council in 1989, can be seen as the decisive document in the preparation of the EMU that was launched with the Maastricht Treaty. The report, on the one hand, "speaks of the necessity of a macroeconomic framework," but, on the other hand, advances an ordoliberal argument for the "budgetary disciplining of national fiscal policies" (Hacker and Koch, p. 15). The report indeed points to "the lack of sufficient convergence of fiscal policies as reflected in large and persistent budget deficits in certain countries" (Delors 1989, p. 8). This is described as something that could be a potential burden for a common monetary policy, which is why an economic and monetary union would "require a high degree of compatibility of economic policies and consistency in a number of other policy areas, particularly in the fiscal field" (Delors 1989, p. 13). The document acknowledges that the budget of the EU would be relatively small compared to the overall public spending in the union on national and local levels. Which is why it concludes "that the task of setting a Community-wide fiscal policy stance will have to be performed through the coordination of national budgetary policies" (Delors 1989, p. 20). Such arrangements would enable the

EU to establish "a coherent mix of fiscal and monetary policies" (Delors 1989, p. 21).

The measures taken in the field of monetary policy leading up to the EMU, especially the snake agreement and the EMS, show that monetary integration had to some extent already happened in the EC before the introduction of the euro. However, the Maastricht Treaty of 1992 took monetary integration to a whole new level. The treaty states the goal of the creation of an EMU and defines the different stages in the process leading up to the introduction of a common currency. This involved the creation of new institutions such as the European Central Bank System (ECBS), the European Central Bank (ECB) (Article 4a) and the European Monetary Institute (EMI) (Article 109f) (Treaty on European Union 1992). In addition to this institutional framework the treaty introduced certain convergence criteria (Article 109j) that a country had to meet which wanted to join the European currency union. These included "the achievement of a high degree of price stability," "the sustainability of the government financial position," "the observance of the normal fluctuation margins provided for by the exchange-rate mechanism of the European Monetary System, for at least two years, without devaluing against the currency of any other Member State," and "the durability of convergence achieved by the Member State and of its participation in the exchange-rate mechanism of the European Monetary System being reflected in the long-term interest rate levels" (Article 109j) (Treaty on European Union 1992, p. 41). In adopting these provisions, the Maastricht treaty adopted the Delors Report as a blueprint for economic and monetary integration in the EU. It also laid out the plan for the different stages that had to be reached in the implementation process and therein again followed the Delors Report.

The parties to the Maastricht Treaty were very careful to separate monetary integration from fiscal integration, and reduce common fiscal policy to the minimum absolutely necessary for the functioning of the EU. With the convergence criteria the document also included strict rules to ensure budgetary discipline among the governments of the member states and to deter any attempt at free-riding of individual countries at the expense of other countries. In article 1 of the *Protocol on the Excessive Deficit Procedure*, which is a Protocol to the Maastricht Treaty, reference values are specified that shall not be exceeded by any member country. This includes a threshold of 3 percent for the ratio of the government deficit (actual or planned) to GDP and a threshold of 60 percent for the ratio of government debt to GDP (Treaty on European Union 1992).[1] These reference values serve the Commission in its task of monitoring budgetary discipline of the individual members states which is described in article 104c of the treaty. Article 104c explicitly states: "The Commission shall monitor the development of the budgetary situation and of the stock of government debt in the Member States with a view to identifying gross errors." (Treaty on European Union 1992, p. 27) Article 104c in connection with the *Protocol on the Excessive Deficit Procedure* also describes the actions which the Commission may take in concert with the European Council if the government of a member state is culpable of such gross errors. The thresholds stipulated for government debt clearly show the concerns of the member states about the stability of the EMU and the possible lack of budgetary discipline in some member countries. They also speak to

1 Other elements of the convergence criteria not directly concerning fiscal policy focused on price stability, exchange rate stability, and long-term interest rates for sovereign bonds. In the field of price stability, a threshold of 1.5 percent above the average of the three countries with the lowest inflation rates was set, measured by the Harmonized Index of Consumer Prices (HICP), an indicator of price stability for the ECB. It was also decided that the exchange rate of a country that wants to join the EMU should not have been devalued over the previous two years and the currency of the respective country should generally be deemed stable. For the long-term interest rates of 10-year government bonds a threshold of two percent above the average of the three member states with the lowest inflation (again measured by HICP) was set.

the focus of the foundation of the EMU which was clearly on the stability of monetary integration and much less concerned with a common fiscal policy. This was especially confirmed by the Stability and Growth Pact (SGP) with the measures of multilateral budgetary surveillance which it put in place. After Maastricht and with the following treaties of the EU, fiscal integration remained largely off the table, and for the most part fiscal policy stayed a national matter. Section 3 will look deeper into the level of fiscal integration that has been reached to date in the EU.

In economics the leading theory on monetary union is the theory of Optimal Currency Area (OCA). It is interesting to see that this theory had only little impact, if any, on the formation of the EMU and the convergence criteria (Arestis and Sawyer 2011). Which means that the undertaking of introducing a common currency can primarily be seen as a political project and much less as an economic one. In this context, it is interesting to note that none of the major contributions to this theory – neither the early publications by Robert A. Mundell (1961) and Ronald I. McKinnon (1963) nor the later "new OCA theory" – include any deeper elaboration or conceptualization of the meaning which fiscal policy has for monetary integration. An exception is Francesco Paolo Mongelli, who analyzed the relationship of OCA to the EMU. He treated the pro-cyclicality of fiscal policy in the EU as a problem and came to the conclusion that "fiscal integration [...] is likely to play an increasingly supportive role for the functioning of EMU" (Mongelli 2008, p. 52). But overall, fiscal policy can be seen as a blind spot of OCA theory, which restricts its explanatory power. There are other reasons to question the value of this theory, especially, its failure to provide proper explanations for the functioning of the few real-world cases of regional currency unions that exist today. It was not least the euro crisis which demonstrated the limitations of this theoretical approach.

The Need for the Coordination of Monetary and Fiscal Policy

Monetary and fiscal Policy in the EU are highly interconnected and there are several potential spill-over effects from one policy field into the other (Šehović 2014). These spill-overs can potentially have both positive and negative impacts on the economic performance of individual members states in the EU and of the EU as a whole. Which leads us to the conclusion that the coordination of these two different types of policy is indispensable. This study holds that deeper integration in the fiscal field would make such coordination easier, because it would involve the creation of an institutional layer that is on par with the ECB, which has the undivided responsibility for the monetary policy of the EU, whereas fiscal policy is the sole responsibility of the individual member states. Damir Šehović (2014, p. 70) described this as the "division of jurisdiction between the national and supranational authority within the EMU, i.e. the existence of many individual fiscal authorities and only one monetary authority." It is not suggested here to replace the many individual fiscal authorities by a supranational fiscal authority, but to complement them by such an authority.

The devastating impacts, which negative spill-overs from one policy field into the other can have, were on full display during the euro crisis. One of the major design flaws of the EMU, as devised with the Maastricht Treaty and the SGP, was the strict separation of these two fields which was implemented under the assumption that full monetary integration is possible while leaving the responsibility of fiscal policy in the hands of the governments of the individual member states. The interconnectedness between these two fields is best demonstrated when looking at the long-term yields for sovereign bonds of each individual member country. In the run-up to the euro crisis there was a remarkable convergence in the level of these yields for all member states of the euro zone (Havertz 2013). But when the 2008 global financial crisis struck, investors realized that they may have been overly confident in the ability of some of the financially weaker countries of the euro zone, namely of Greece, Ireland, Italy, Portugal, and Spain to pay off the debt they had taken on when they gave out these bonds. The result was a wide spread of bond yields with excessively high rates for these countries. Whereas other countries such as Germany, France, the Netherlands, and Finland benefitted from decreasing bond yields. Which meant that these countries could now borrow at even lower costs (Havertz 2013). The crisis ensued when some of the countries of the European periphery were not anymore able to refinance their debt, which had manyfold effects, one of them was the considerable weakening of the exchange rate of the euro against other major currencies.

But more importantly, it was some of the design flaws of the EMU that made the euro crisis possible – without them this crisis may not have happened. It turned out that the institutional design of the EMU with its strong focus on price stability and the separation of monetary and fiscal policy had actually contributed to the crisis; and the measures taken for crisis mitigation perpetuated the problems which caused the crisis in the first place. Thus, the very measures taken to confront the crisis made the crisis even worse. As Björn Hacker (2013, p. 2) notes correctly, "the only take on the crisis officially recognised by the EU institutions had been the transgressions of individual Member States against European regulations and the latters' ineffectiveness." Even as it had become apparent that the crisis had other main causes and deeper roots, the focus of the "stability camp" (Hacker and Koch 2017, p. 4) remained on measures of austerity in the countries that were mainly affected by the crisis. This involved "continuing unchanged demands made to crisis-countries Cyprus, Greece, Ireland, Portugal and Spain to lower wage costs, cut social services and implement privatization" (Hacker 2013, p. 2). The stability camp was and still is led by Germany which is very reluctant to get engaged in the coordination of economic policies, not to speak of deeper fiscal integration.

As Sebastian Dullien and Ulrike Guerot (2012, p. 3) noted in an influential policy brief for the *European Council on Foreign Relations*, "from a German point of view, no co-ordination is needed as long as everyone has the correct policies." It was the German government, especially the then powerful minister of finance, Wolfgang Schäuble, who made German influence being felt in Europe and led the euro zone on a course of crisis mitigation that primarily focused on austerity, which meant for the countries that were most severely affected by the crisis, that they were led down the path toward deflation. The stability camp led by Germany was particularly opposed to "two possible solutions to the euro crisis that were proposed by others in Europe: Eurobonds and the idea of turning the ECB into a lender of last resort for the eurozone along the lines of the US Federal Reserve" (Dullien and Guerot 2012, p. 2). According to Dullien and Guerot (2012), the German focus on austerity was not only owed to the experience which Germany had made with hyperinflation during the Weimar Republic, as has often been argued in defense of these policies, or to the simple pursuit of national interests. The German preference for these policies had much deeper roots in ordoliberalism, a particular strand of neoliberalism, which provided the ideological basis for the social market economy of West Germany after the Second World War.

Ordoliberalism is different from the Anglo-Saxon neoliberalism of the Chicago School which emerged in the 1970s in that it proposes a framework for the economy set by government which spells out the basic rules according to which market participants are expected to operate. This role of the government is alien to Anglo-Saxon neoliberalism because the latter claims "the superiority of economic freedom over public intervention" (Young 2017, p. 35) and as such has much more in common with the classical liberalism of the 19th century and early 20th century. When the EU negotiated the terms of crisis mitigation, the stability camp was very reluctant to make any concessions that might lead to a loose monetary policy or a more deeply integrated fiscal policy (Hacker 2013). Even after the experience with the crisis, fiscal policy remained largely the responsibility of the individual member states. The measures taken to address the crisis did not deepen fiscal integration in any significant way, this is true for the Six-Pack, the Two-Pack and also for the Fiscal Compact of 2013. "The Compact did not in any way change the structure of subsidiarity, nor did it change the position of fiscal policy within the governance structure of the EMU. It hardened its structure and reinforced its resolve." (Bonefeld 2017, p. 140) Peter Nedergaard (2013, p. 20) also observed that with the Fiscal Compact "the rules of public debt have been strengthened." This is a development which he attributes to the strong influence of ordoliberalism on the decision-making of the EU.

From an ordoliberal point of view, the most important element of the Maastricht Treaty for the guaranteeing of the credibility of the common currency and the strengthening of fiscal discipline was the no-bailout clause, which is included in article 104b of the treaty. It states explicitly that neither the EU nor any member state shall be "liable for or assume the commitments of central governments, regional, local or other public authorities, other bodies governed by public law, or public undertakings of another Member State, without prejudice to mutual financial guarantees for the joint execution of a specific project" (Treaty on

European Union 1992, p. 27). This provision in the treaty protected the EU and any individual member states from responsibility for the debt of a member state of the EU. Which means that the EU was designed in a way that individual member states could enjoy the benefits of trade integration and of monetary integration without having to concern themselves with the fallout which integration in these fields may have for individual member states with large current account deficits and high levels of unemployment.

The ECB as an independent central bank was intentionally designed to preclude the "co-ordination of fiscal and monetary policy, [and] has also disabled the central banking system from providing sufficient support to national governments and their budget deficits" (Arestis and Sawyer 2011, p. 31). However, despite the fact that the no-bailout clause expressly forbids it to take on the liabilities of the governments of individual member states, the ECB, led by Mario Draghi has implemented a bond purchasing scheme which secured the debt of member states in crisis. The ECB de facto took on the role as lender of last resort, which the Maastricht Treaty was designed to prevent. This courageous policy is likely to have saved Greece from bankruptcy and the euro zone from falling apart. It also attests to the need of a reform of the EMU and the limitations which the Maastricht Treaty has set for the coordination of fiscal and monetary policy and for fiscal integration in the EU.

Prospects of Fiscal Integration in the EU

Proponents of fiscal integration in the EU hold that monetary policy cannot be pursued on union level without some integration in the field of fiscal policy. So far fiscal integration has largely been prevented by the *stability camp* which fears that a common fiscal policy will be detrimental to the stability of the common currency. But recently several proposals have been put on the table for ways in which deeper integration in the field of fiscal policy can be achieved in the EU. This section looks into these proposals and reflects on whether an independent fiscal policy on union level involving the right to taxation is a possible scenario for the future of the EU. After all, this would be a necessary step in the process of European integration if the member countries of the EU ever plan to reach the highest stage of regional integration that is aimed at the creation of a political union.

Proposals for a fiscal union include three core ideas. 1. The introduction of common debt liability at union level which would involve the replacement of sovereign bonds on national level by long-term bonds issued by the ECB, or by any other debt agency that would yet have to be created. 2. The establishment of an EU-wide fiscal transfer system that could be used to stimulate economies of member states that are affected by negative demand shocks (Hacker and Koch 2017). This may also involve the creation of a European unemployment scheme that functions as an automatic stabilizer for the economies of member countries in cases where they are affected by asymmetric shocks. 3. The completion of the Banking Union, which would provide more stability to the financial system of individual member states and to the EU as a whole. I will in the following examine these proposals in more detail and also look at some reports that have recently been released by the leaders of European political and economic institutions on the future of the EMU.

The problems which the euro zone faced during the euro crisis primarily resulted from the fact that it has a common monetary policy while each country pursues its individual fiscal policy, involving the issuing of their individual sovereign bonds. But in the aftermath of the global financial crisis of 2008, these sovereign bonds proved to be vulnerable to changing patterns of risk perception and notions of credibility. This especially affected countries of the so-called European periphery where the yields for sovereign bonds increased dramatically during the euro crisis. Such problems with risk perception and notions of credibility (or the lack thereof) could be avoided with pooled and centrally managed bonds for the whole euro area. Such euro bonds would involve shared liability and the partial integration of fiscal policy for all member countries of the euro zone. In the long-term, shared debt responsibility would allow to do away with the no-bailout clause of the Maastricht Treaty (article 104b). All countries would benefit from this scheme – the weaker countries as well as the economically stronger countries of the EU. It would prove advantageous for the weaker countries to participate in a system of sovereign bonds that is led by strong countries with a good fiscal and financial position. They would share in the credibility of these countries and in the lower risk perception that concern their individual bonds (Havertz 2013). Hence, it is much more likely that the strong countries would lift up the weaker countries in this regard than that the weaker countries would drag the stronger countries down to their level. Stronger countries such as Germany, the Netherlands, Austria, or Finland would have to accept a modest hike in yields for long term sovereign bonds when switching from national sovereign bonds to eurobonds. But in exchange for the acceptance of this small hike they would gain a fiscally and financially more stable euro zone (Havertz 2013).

We can distinguish two different phases of the debate on euro bonds. The first phase occurred during the euro crisis when a number of economists and politicians reacted to the crisis and included proposals for the introduction of euro bonds into their conceptions. The second phase started with a *Reflection Paper* which was published by the European Commission in May 2017 (European Commission 2017) and the reactions to the proposals made in this document. In the first phase there were several proposals which had different features and which can primarily be distinguished regarding the degree of common debt responsibility which they involved. One of the most discussed – and at the same time least specific – proposals was that of Jean-Claude Juncker and Giulio Tremonti (2010), who suggested the transition from national bonds to euro bonds through a gradual process of the exchange of national bonds into euro bonds.

Jacques Delpla and Jakob von Weizsäcker (2010) made a proposal for euro bonds which they called "blue bonds." It was conceptualized as a layered instrument with two tranches, one blue, one red. In the blue tranche all member countries of the euro zone would pool their debt up to 60 percent of their GDP. The red tranche would include all other sovereign debt, i.e. all debt exceeding the threshold of 60 percent of a member country's GDP. Delpla and von Weizäcker's proposal had clear advantages. The separation of bonds into two tranches, a European and a national one, made sure that individual member countries could still borrow at their own discretion, while the pooling of the debt of all countries of up to 60 percent of their GDP meant that their fiscal policy would be provided with a strong anchor. This was a proposal likely to provide high levels of liquidity and strengthen fiscal discipline at the same time. The major disadvantage of this proposal was the potential exposure to market pressures for the remaining national debt. This disadvantage would accrue from fiscal integration being only partial and not covering all of the debt of each member country.

Paul De Grauwe and Wim Moesen (2009) favored an approach that would give the responsibility for the management of euro bonds to the European Investment Bank (EIB) and with this step put the bank into the position of a European debt agency. This proposal included the idea that individual member countries should pay the same interest rates for euro bonds which they had paid for their national bonds before switching from these to euro bonds. This procedure to determine the interest rate which an individual country would have to pay is problematic, because "markets would price in this switch" and euro bonds may thus "inherit a potentially distorted price" (Havertz 2013, p. 75). Wim Boonstra (2010; 2011) suggested the complete replacement of national long-term sovereign bonds by euro bonds. His proposal also included the creation of an "EMU fund" the purpose of which would be to issue the bonds and distribute the money raised this way to the individual member states. The interests which countries would have to pay were supposed to be calculated based on the financial position of a country at the time it was taking the money. This proposal was very bold because it involved the total shift of debt responsibility from the national to the European level.

Each of these early proposals for euro bonds would involve a more integrated fiscal policy, but the degree of fiscal integration would vary, depending on the level of responsibility given to the debt agency handling the bonds. While there were several proponents of euro bonds, the idea has not gained traction in political circles of the EU, especially because of the strong opposition to it in the stability camp. German chancellor, Angela Merkel, had famously declared that euro bonds would not be introduced "as long as I live" (Isenson 2012), seemingly precluding the creation of such bonds as long as she has any say in German politics – and European politics for that matter. As will be treated later, this rigid position of Merkel toward common sovereign bonds had somewhat softened in the face of the economic crisis caused by the Covid-19 pandemic.

Since the end of the euro crisis, some positions that were opposed to the integration of fiscal policy on European level have yielded. The realization has sunk in that explanations for the euro crisis which solely focus on the irresponsible behavior of public debtors in the European periphery are falling short of grasping the causes of the crisis to their full extent. These insights have recently revived the debate about euro bonds and common debt responsibility. In the *Reflection Paper on the Deepening of the Economic and Monetary Union* of May 2017, the European Commission (2017) acknowledges the benefits that may accrue from the issuance of a common debt instrument. The Commission does not call it euro bonds, probably because the term is fraught with reservations against the concept due to the heated debates during the euro crisis. The Commission instead talks about "safe assets," and compares them to the bonds issued by the US Treasury. The paper explicitly states that these safe assets are conceptualized as sovereign bonds and it adds:

> A European safe asset would be a new financial instrument for the common issuance of debt, which would reinforce integration and financial stability. However, developing a safe asset for the euro area raises a number of complex legal, political and institutional questions that would need to be explored in great detail. The question of debt mutualisation, in particular, is heavily debated, also in light of concerns about weakening incentives for sound national policies (European Commission 2017, p. 22).

This is the first time that a high-profile paper of the European Commission committed to the introduction of sovereign bonds for the euro zone as a whole and highlighted the benefits of such financial instruments for the "integration and financial stability" of the EU. This is a departure from the stance the EU had taken so far which attributed financial stability solely to price stability and fiscal discipline. Whereas this statement on safe assets – while it still emphasizes the need for "sound national policies" – acknowledges that fiscal integration in itself can be a source of financial stability. It also concedes that there still is a long way to go before the debate on euro bonds can come to a conclusion and describes "debt mutualisation" as a particularly contentious issue. After all, the introduction of a safe asset that involves debt mutualization would mean a wholesale break with the no-bailout clause of the Maastricht Treaty. But it appears that for the European Commission the risks involved in the creation of common sovereign bonds appear to be preferable to the risks that accrue from a bond market where each member state issues its own individual bonds. The *Reflection Paper* (2017, p. 22) criticizes this "asymmetric provision of safe assets" with its "heterogenous risk characteristics" and goes on to highlight the risks involved in this setup as follows:

> Experience has shown that at times of stress, the current structure of the sovereign bond market and the large exposure of banks to their national sovereign have amplified market volatility, affecting the stability of the financial sector, with tangible and diversified effects on the real economies of the euro area Member States (European Commission 2017, p. 22).

It appeared that the Commission had learned its lesson from the euro crisis and that reason was prevailing over the prejudices that are rooted in ideological views on sound economy and financial and fiscal stability. However, the obstacles to euro bonds and the many issues that would have to be considered with their introduction have still prevented any serious policy move to refinance national public debt through commonly issued sovereign bonds.

But it appears to have inspired a new debate on the merits

of the proposals for such bonds. In 2018, the European Systemic Risk Board (ESRB) carried out a feasibility study of sovereign bond-backed securities (SBBS). These are private financial instruments which are based on sovereign bonds and involve tranching, i.e. splitting up a bond in at least two tranches, one designated as a senior tranche and the other one as a junior tranche with the senior part normally involving much less risk than the junior tranche. The study comes to the conclusion that "the pooling and tranching of euro area sovereign bonds produces low-risk assets (senior SBBS) that are at least as low-risk as German sovereign bonds" (European Systemic Risk Board [ESRB] 2018, p. 33). But the ESRB also notes that this procedure of issuing bonds could also result in the production of "assets (junior SBBS) which may be riskier than Greek sovereign bonds" (ESRB 2018, p. 33). In a press release from May 2018, the European Commission (2018) backed the idea of SBBS, expressing the conviction that SBBS will be helpful in advancing the completion of the Banking Union and the Capital Markets Union, leading to a deeper EMU. They could reduce risks through enhanced risk diversification by spreading risks more widely across investors and across borders. De Grauwe and Ji (2019) point out that contrary to some of the earlier proposals for euro bonds, the more recent proposals for safe assets or SBBS do not in any way include considerations of common debt liability. In their view, the euro zone cannot be stabilized by mechanisms that trust in the market as a disciplining force. What instead is needed is first, "the willingness of the European Central Bank (ECB) to provide liquidity in the sovereign bond markets of the Eurozone during times of crisis," and, second, the creation of "Eurobonds that are based on joint liability of the participating national governments" (Grauwe and Ji 2019, p. 46). Both steps suggested by de Grauwe and Ji would involve the shift of more sovereignty from the national to the European level and, hence, the willingness of the member states of the EU to go the final step toward a political union.

Álvaro Leandro and Jeromin Zettelmeyer (2019) in their contribution to the debate, discuss three different types of proposals for euro bonds. Firstly, bonds with a senior tranche and a junior tranche, where the senior tranche constitutes the safe asset and the junior tranche is the responsibility of national fiscal authorities quite in keeping with the earlier proposal of Delpla and von Weizsäcker (2010). Secondly, a safe asset that is issued by a "euro area–level fiscal authority" that has "the right to issue debt, within predefined limits, backed by a dedicated revenue stream" (Leandro and Zettelmeyer 2019, p. 2). Their contribution is, thirdly, particularly interested in discussing proposals that involve the creation of "a (senior) financial intermediary, or a regulatory framework for private intermediaries, that would issue debt securities backed by a diversified portfolio of euro area sovereign debt" which they assume is the "only approach that may become politically feasible in the foreseeable future" (Leandro and Zettelmeyer 2019, pp. 2-3).

Nermina Pobrić (2019, p. 25) weighs the pros and cons of all the proposals for euro bonds and comes to the conclusion that "it is not certain whether the introduction of common Eurobonds could bring stability in the euro area or not." But she is convinced that the introduction of euro bonds would face many legal obstacles and a strong political opposition (Pobrić 2019). Even though the debate on euro bonds has been revived recently, and there are now proposals for types of sovereign bond-backed assets that are supported by the European Commission, the pace in which these developments are moving is rather slow; and a final resolution is not yet in sight. What has brought a new dynamic to the debate on euro bonds is the Covid-19 pandemic and the proposals for the financing of the measures which the EU has taken as a relief effort. We will return to this topic in the section on the Covid-19 crisis.

The creation of automatic fiscal stabilizers for the euro zone

Recently, the claim has been made that the creation of an automatic stabilizer for the euro zone would provide a layer of economic security on the level of the euro zone in addition to the layers that exist on national level. In the Five Presidents Report (Juncker et al. 2015)[2] the heads of the five major EU institutions concerned with the EMU stated that the first layer of protection had to be on national level. For this to work, responsible national fiscal policies would be essential. "They must perform a double function: guaranteeing that public debt is sustainable and ensuring that fiscal automatic stabilisers can operate to cushion country-specific economic shocks." (Juncker et al. 2015, p. 14) But the document also emphasized the need to create a second layer of public risk-sharing in the medium term "through a mechanism of fiscal stabilization for the euro area as a whole" (Juncker et al. 2015, p. 4).

The *Reflection Paper* of the European Commission of May 2017 (European Commission 2017, pp. 24-25) is more specific in spelling out the features and conditions of what it calls a "macroeconomic stabilisation function" that would complement the national fiscal stabilizers on euro zone level. It is conceptualized as an instrument to be used in the event of a severe asymmetric shock, because such a shock is the most likely event to strain monetary policy beyond its limits. As a key principle the Reflection Paper emphasizes that "the function should not lead to permanent transfers, minimise moral hazard, and not duplicate the role of the European Stability Mechanism (ESM) as crisis management tool" (European Commission 2017, p. 25). Interestingly, this instrument is supposed to be open to all member states of the EU and not just to the members of the euro zone. This would

2 The five presidents included the presidents 5of the European Commission, the European Council, the European Parliament, the ECB, and the president of the Eurogroup.

guarantee that all countries of the EU could be supported in the event of an asymmetric shock. This stabilization function could be established through the creation of a "fiscal capacity" for the EU. For the financing of this function several sources have been taken into consideration, for instance, "national contributions based on a share of GDP or a share of VAT, or revenues from excises, levies or corporate taxes" (European Commission 2017, pp. 25-26). The Commission identified two main areas that should be covered by the stabilization function: "The protection of public investment from economic downturn and an unemployment insurance scheme in cases of a sudden rise of unemployment level." (European Commission 2017, p. 26.)

Securing these two areas with a union-wide fiscal capacity could make a strong contribution to the restoration of stability in a country that is in need of financial assistance. Investment protection would make sure that important public investment is secured in times of asymmetric shocks and would thus prevent national fiscal policy from turning pro-cyclical. An unemployment reinsurance scheme could make sure that countries that are hit by crises could keep handing out unemployment benefits on an appropriate level and thus not only support the livelihoods of those who lost their jobs but also secure high levels of aggregate demand. Such an unemployment reinsurance scheme could therefore function as an automatic stabilizer on European level. Stabilizing national economies that are affected by asymmetric shocks or rising unemployment may not only be beneficial for these individual economies but also protect the rest of the union from the fallout of these developments.

Both the securitization of public investments of individual member states as well as the unemployment reinsurance scheme as suggested by the European Commission do not constitute the bold approach that is needed to secure fiscal stability for the union as a whole in the long run. Instead, it appears that the Commission has adopted what has been termed a strategy of small steps (De Grauwe and Ji 2019; see also Enderlein et al. 2012). Only if further steps were to follow, this strategy could indeed one day result in a higher degree of fiscal integration in the EU.

The completion of the Banking Union

The Banking Union is a result of the deteriorating credit conditions in the countries of the euro zone during the euro crisis. It was acknowledged that bank supervision had to be centralized on European level in order to put banks in the EU on a more secure financial footing. In the discussions on the creation of the Banking Union there had again been two camps who advanced their arguments along the lines of the division between those favoring a stability union and those promoting a fiscal union, or as Thorsten Beck and Hans-Helmut Kotz (2017, p. 109) put it, the "rule-based versus a discretionary approach." However, Germany, as the country that is leading the group in favor of a stability union was ready to make some pragmatic compromises in the creation of the Banking Union (Feld, Köhler, and Nienstedt 2017), which eventually allowed to introduce the two main initiatives of that union with the Single Supervisory Mechanism (SSM) and Single Resolution Mechanism (SRM). Germany's support for these pillars of the Banking Union should not be surprising, since the creation of an institutional framework that allows for rule-based European governance is at the very heart of the German ordoliberal approach to European integration (Skalkos 2018).

With the SSM, which was established in 2014, the ECB became the top supervisory authority for all banks in the euro zone. It now directly supervises 113 banks in the members states of the euro zone, which account for 82 percent of the banking assets in these countries (ECB n.d.-a). With its supervisory function the

ECB only concentrates on banks which it deems significant, i.e. larger banks that account for a large amount of the banking assets in the respective countries and who are considered important for the financial systems of these countries. Smaller banks are still supervised by national authorities. But even for these smaller banks the ECB is the ultimate supervisory authority. The SSM works in conjunction with the SRM, which is the second pillar of the Banking Union. Both are based on a single rule book for banking supervision in the EU. According to the ECB (n.d.-b), the purpose of the SRM is "to ensure the efficient resolution of failing banks with minimal costs for taxpayers and to the real economy." The ECB has the authority to decide whether a bank is failing or likely to fail.

The importance which banks and their potential failure can have for the fiscal policies of an individual member country has become clear during the euro crisis. The possible default of a government on its debt may have severe consequences for the banks in the financial system of the respective country. "When the sovereign is pushed into a bad equilibrium it becomes very likely that the domestic banks will experience solvency problems because they are the major holders of the sovereign bonds." (De Grauwe and Ji 2018, p. 6) As de Grauwe and Ji observed, it is equally possible that a sovereign debt crisis originates from a banking crisis: "A domestic banking crisis forces the sovereign to step in to save the banking system. This typically requires the government to take on more debt thereby creating a risk of insolvency." (De Grauwe and Ji 2018, p. 6) Due to this deep interconnectedness of the banking system with the system of sovereign debt on the individual country level, it makes sense for a bloc of states with a common monetary policy to combine the common supervision of the bank systems of these states with some level of common responsibility for the debt amounted in these systems.

The Banking Union has so far missed to go this last step of coordination between monetary and fiscal policy. Most observers of the integration in this field of financial policy agree that the Banking Union has not yet be completed in some important respects (De Grauwe and Ji 2018; Hacker and Koch 2017). According to de Grauwe and Ji (2018), this concerns the common resolution of failed banks as well as common deposit insurance. They criticized that the common resolution has only been partly implemented while common deposit insurance is non-existent in the framework of the Banking Union and attributed these shortcomings to the fact that the stability camp still has the upper hand in matters of fiscal policy on union level.

The Covid-19 Relief Package and Fiscal Policy

When the euro crisis hit in 2009 and several scholars and politicians discussed the creation of euro bonds as a measure of crisis mitigation, Charles Wyplosz (2011, p. 15) remarked that "crises often offer an opportunity to move lines," but also warned that such moves may sometimes go in a direction opposite to the one intended. In 2020, the EU again faced a crisis with the Covid-19 pandemic which brought the health systems of some of its member countries to the brink of collapse and caused a severe economic downturn. The question arose whether this new crisis offered another opportunity for euro bonds to be considered as a measure for the stabilization of the euro zone (Thomadakis 2020). There are almost no scholarly studies on the potentials of euro bonds as a measure to counter the financial and fiscal pressures exerted by the Covid-19 crisis. Which is why this study had to rely primarily on media reports and on official documents and press releases of EU institutions such as the European Commission, the European Council, and the ECB.

With the Covid-19 crisis the political leaders in the capitals of Europe as well as in Brussels realized that the member countries could not be left alone with the response to the social, economic, and financial challenges of the crisis; and the EU had to take on a role in supporting the economies of the countries that were most hardly affected by the pandemic. As Dominic Clark (2020) noted, "governments are going to find it even harder to balance budgets and will need to increase borrowing significantly." Only a few weeks after the onset of the crisis another debate was sparked about the issuance of euro bonds as a means to finance the Covid-19 relief measures and bolster the fiscal policies of the individual member states. Most vocal among the proponents of euro bonds or "coronavirus bonds" was Italian Prime Minister Giuseppe Conte (Nienaber 2020). Conte claimed that either such bonds had to be created or, alternatively, a European guarantee fund. This call was swiftly dismissed by German chancellor Merkel as well as by her minister of economics Peter Altmaier (Chazan 2020).

However, with the lingering of the crisis, positions on the common financing of the relief effort - involving some form of fiscal integration - started to move, and the opposition to it weakened. Notably, two influential German economists, Michael Hüther and Achim Truger, the latter a member of the Council of Economic Experts which advises the German government, started to back the issuance of European crisis bonds (Chazan 2020). Gradually, Merkel also warmed up to the idea of EU bonds to finance the measures for coronavirus relief. But it was important to her to ensure that any measures taken were of temporary nature and that they did not violate the no-bailout clause that was introduced with the Maastricht Treaty. Merkel suggested that the legal basis for such measures could be article 122 (2) of the EU treaties, the so-called solidarity clause, which allowed individual member countries to guarantee the government bonds of other member countries and to finance specific forms of financial assistance on EU level (Von der Burchard, 2020).

Eventually, the measures which the EU adopted did involve commonly issued bonds. Germany in tandem with France suggested to make grants to those member countries most severely affected by the pandemic. These grants were supposed to be financed through bonds issued by the European Commission and repaid by the EU budget (Delfs, Nussbaum, and Kuzmanovic 2020). Merkel even signaled that she was open to use this type of financing again in the future, should the need arise. For the time being, the issuance of euro bonds as a general means of fiscal policy for all member states is off the table. But it is noteworthy that the debate moved in the direction of the acceptance of common debt responsibility despite the no-bailout clause. Whereas Germany was the country which was blocking any attempt to pursue the mutualization of debt in the euro zone and mainly responsible for the imposition of austerity in exchange for the solidarity shown to the main debtor countries during the euro crisis, it was not so much Germany anymore that was opposed. But there was another group of frugals with the Netherlands, Austria, Denmark, and Sweden, who had to be convinced to provide guarantees for money granted to other member states (Delfs, Nussbaum, and Kuzmanovic 2020).

The measures which EU leaders finally agreed on are impressive. In March 2020, the ECB initiated an emergency program of 750 billion euros which included another bond buying scheme in addition to that already under way. This program was increased by another 600 billion euros in June 2020 (European Council 2020). At the end of 2020, EU leaders agreed on the scope of the Multiannual Fiscal Framework for the period 2021-2027 which accounted for 1,074.3 billion euros and was supposed to support investments in the digital and green future of Europe. They decided that another 540 billion euros should be used for safety nets that support workers, businesses and the individual member states as well. Taken together this spending effort amounted to 2,364.3 billion euros (European Council 2020).

One important element of this relief package is the *Support to Mitigate Unemployment Risks in an Emergency* (SURE) which is designated to support jobs and workers and to help European citizens keep their jobs during the coronavirus crisis. SURE is funded with 100 billion euros, 90.3 billion euros of which had already been applied for by 18 member countries altogether, and 39.5 billion euro of which had been disbursed as of December 1, 2020 (European Council 2020). According to the European Commission (2020), "SURE is a crucial element of the EU's comprehensive strategy to protect citizens and mitigate the severely negative socio-economic consequences of the coronavirus pandemic." The loans provided by this program are guaranteed by individual member states on a voluntary basis. SURE is financed through "social bonds" with an optional 5-, 10- or 15-year maturity which are issued by the European Commission. Since October 27, 2020, these bonds were listed at the Luxemburg Stock Exchange. At the end of 2020, the Commission proudly announced that "there was very strong investor interest in these highly rated instruments, and the oversubscription resulted in favourable pricing terms for the bonds" (European Commission 2020). After all, the European Union now is issuing common bonds, but only temporary and not as part of a regular scheme of common debt responsibility.

Conclusion

As a response to the Covid-19 crisis, the EU has finally agreed to issue common social bonds. While these measures are of a temporary nature, they show that deeper integration in the field of fiscal policy is possible. Several authors have made the case that integration is not only possible but an absolute necessity, if the EU wants to put its social, financial and economic systems on a stable footing. It has become clear that integration in this policy area has the potential to bring more and not less stability to the EU. Some economists and politicians who after the euro crisis have been firmly in the camp of those in favor of a stability union have recently become more open to proposals for more cooperation in the field of fiscal policy and for more coordination of fiscal and monetary policies. Whereas there has been some movement toward deeper fiscal integration, those advocating a stability union are still reluctant to give up the no-bailout clause of the Maastricht Treaty because they fear that moral hazard may result from this step. However, if the EU wants to go the last steps in the process of integration toward a political union, moving forward with a common fiscal policy will be inevitable. This does not mean that the individual member states would have to give up their sovereignty in this policy field completely, as was necessary with monetary policy. On the contrary, the sharing of competences between national and supranational level is quite possible and desirable in the area of fiscal policy.

Chapter 6

The Treaty of Amsterdam
A Transitional Treaty

Introduction

The Treaty of Amsterdam was signed on October 2, 1997, came into force on May 1, 1999, and the negotiations of the treaty lasted for about two years, from June 1995 to June 1997 (European Commission 1999a). The treaty is an agreement of the European Union (EU) that was primarily intended to initiate the reform of the institutional structure and decision-making processes of the EU. The document comprises "13 Protocols, 51 Declarations adopted by the Conference and 8 Declarations by Member States plus amendments to the existing Treaties set out in 15 Articles" (ibid.). Since the Single European Act of 1986 and the Maastricht Treaty of 1992 had already brought about significant changes for the EU only a few years earlier, the question can be raised why another treaty was deemed necessary at this point of time. There were several issues that required further adjustment and regulation, particularly with the European currency union that was about to be established and with the considerable enlargement of the EU that was expected to happen with the accession of several

Central and Eastern European countries to the EU.

The Treaty of Amsterdam sought to modernize the EU's institutional framework by giving the European Parliament and the Court of Justice more authority (Due, 1998). It also further expanded the use of qualified majority voting (QMV) in the Council of Ministers (Moravscik and Nicolaidis 1999). The treaty made some significant changes to the Treaty on European Union in the areas of justice and home affairs, foreign and security policy, and in the strengthening of fundamental rights of EU citizens. Moreover, the document introduced a higher level of flexibility through new provisions that made it easier for the member countries to cooperate in specific policy areas (Stubb 1998). Overall, the changes brought about by the Treaty of Amsterdam were not as comprehensive and profound as those that came with the previous two treaties. The provisions of the Treaty of Amsterdam also were less controversial (Moravscik and Nicolaidis 1999). The institutional and procedural changes that were introduced by this treaty will be briefly outlined in the second section of this chapter. This is followed by an analysis of the meaning which the Treaty of Amsterdam had for the economic integration of the European Community. The progress which the treaty provided for in this political-economic process is the main focus of this study.

Major Institutional and Procedural Changes

There were a number of institutional changes which the Intergovernmental Conference (IGC) was tasked to negotiate in the run-up to the signing of the Treaty of Amsterdam in the period 1996-97. In some areas an agreement could be reached, in others the ICG was less successful in forging a consensus among the member states. This study gives an overview of the main institutional and procedural changes which the Treaty of Amsterdam introduced to the European treaties and it also highlights where the EU failed to come to an agreement on such change.

One of the major institutional developments following the Treaty of Amsterdam involved the strengthening of the role of the European Parliament (EP). Due to the changes that have been made to the powers of the EP over decades, the parliament has developed from a consultative parliament to one with ever greater powers (Nentwich and Falkner 1997). Notwithstanding the Amsterdam Treaty's absence of a single, unified decision-making process, notable advancements were achieved. The Maastricht Treaty already established co-decision as a decision procedure of the EU, and it was later extended. Although it was then and still is today not yet the accepted practice for all legislative decisions, co-decision has become more and more accepted as the standard, with cooperation or consultation being considered as the exception (ibid.).

The EP has also been endowed with new powers, including the ability to accede to decisions made by the Council over a member state's violation of Union principles. Nevertheless, the EP's influence in many areas of policy, such as monetary, agricultural, and foreign policy, is still restricted to consultative status (ibid.). By requiring the EP to approve the nominee for Commission President and the College of Commissioners, the treaty also strengthened the role of the European Parliament (EP) in the nomination process (European Commission 1999b). Another important revision was made with Article 137 of the Treaty of Amsterdam, which set a cap to the number of the members of the EP with a maximum number of 700 seats (Piris and Maganza 1998). As Alain Guggenbühl (1997) noted, it was likely at the time that this cap had to go through further revisions with the accession of a larger group of Central and Eastern European countries that was expected to happen at the beginning of the new millennium. The revision of the powers of the EP in the decision-making process of the EU were meant to address the democratic deficit of the bloc and to provide the representatives of the European citizens in this institution with more power to influence decisions made by the Council together with the EP (Moravscik and Nicolaidis 1998).

The Treaty of Amsterdam also gave national parliaments the ability to examine legislative ideas before the Council voted on them. Under the new rules all documents prepared by the European Commission and especially its proposals for legislation had to be submitted to the parliaments of the member states. Upon reception the parliaments were given six weeks to respond and express their views on the respective matters in order to give their views to the Council before any decision was made in that institution (European Commission 1999b).

The decision-making procedures of the EU were also changed through an extension of qualified majority voting (QMV) in the Council. However, it appears that these changes have fallen short of the European Commission's expectations. QMV was only extended to areas that were largely considered uncontroversial. When it comes to QMV, the treaty left the more sensitive areas untouched, wherever substantial national interests would have been affected. In the description of Moravscik and Nicolaidis (1999), the governments of several countries went into the negotiations of the treaty with a long list of national preferences for the extension or rejection of QMV. This resulted in a situation where only limited progress could be made on a meaningful extension of QMV.

> In the end, the Amsterdam Treaty extended QMV to 14 areas, most of them relatively uncontroversial. These included public health, openness, countering fraud, statistics, creation of an advisory body on data protection, outermost regions and customs co-operation. [...] The ten major areas remaining under unanimity were all extremely sensitive

> for one or (more generally) a majority of Member States (free movement of peoples, social security, professional services, indirect taxation, culture, industry, some environmental policies, financial regulation, social policy, and employment incentives). (Moravscik and Nicolaidis 1999, 77)

Overall, the changes brought about by the Treaty of Amsterdam in this area have fallen well short of expectations. This especially pertains to the Commissions failure to amend Article 113 of the Treaty to expand QMV to services trade. Andrew Moravscik and Kalypso Nicolaidis (1999) concluded that, the discussions on QMV did not lead to substantial changes in this area.

Nevertheless, QMV has been extended to the EU's common foreign and security policy (CFSP). But this extension was limited to decisions where the Council of Ministers was tasked with implementing a common strategy that had already been agreed upon by the European Council (European Commission 1999b). In addition, a CFSP High Representative was appointed, who can essentially be seen as the foreign minister of the EU. The title High Representative for Common Foreign and Security Policy was adopted for this position (ibid.). The portfolio of this commissioner was later extended by the Lisbon Treaty which assigned new competences to the holder of this office, for instance, serving as Vice-President of the European Commission.

Another important change brought about by the Treaty of Amsterdam was the movement of many Pillar III concerns, within the pillar structure that was created by the Maastricht Treaty, to Pillar I. This "communitarization" included topics such as border control, immigration, and refugee protection (Inoue 2011). This meant that now community rules would apply to areas like asylum, immigration, and the issuance of visas, which can be seen as a significant step ahead in the process of shifting competences from the member states to the EU (Piris and Marganza 1998). Moravscik and Nicolaidis (1998, 30) noted that this progress in the area of communitarization "was possible only by granting broad opt-outs and flexibility to Britain, Ireland, and Denmark." Britain and Ireland opted out from the Schengen Agreement that was incorporated into the European treaties with the Amsterdam Treaty and provided for new freedom of movement of individuals in Europe. This topic is covered more broadly below. Denmark was granted a similar opt-out that expanded even further by adding all decisions that have an impact on defense (Moravscik and Nicolaidis 1998).

Additionally, the Amsterdam Treaty encouraged closer cooperation across member states, permitting groupings of states to work together on particular projects without compromising fundamental EU values. This made it possible for the majority of member states to act jointly and utilize the EU's institutions and processes for this aim, ultimately expanding European integration while maintaining flexibility (Bär et al. 2000).

Despite the many institutional and procedural changes which the Treaty of Amsterdam engendered for the EU, several scholars and many in the press have described the document as lacking in substance and even as a "failure" (see Guggenbühl 1998; Moravscik and Nicolaidis 1998). One of the major reasons for this assessment is the failure of the EU concerning the reweighting of votes in the Council. This was seen as a necessary precondition for the accession of the states from Central and Eastern Europe which were about to become members of the EU (Spruyt and Lyons 2000). There had been fears among the larger states of the EU that those new states could form a voting bloc and outnumber the larger states in the decision-making process of the Council (ibid.). The issue was later addressed with a reweighting of votes through the Treaty of Nice (Havertz 2022). That was a decision taken just in time before the large accession round of 2004, when ten new member states joined the EU.

The Political-Economic Dimension

One of the major changes with political-economic relevance which the Amsterdam Treaty made to the EC Treaty was the inclusion of new provisions on employment. The concluding parties highlighted it as a substantive amendment to the treaty. It can be tracked in several sections of the Treaty of Amsterdam, starting with Article B which had been changed accordingly and in Article 2 which now stated that the EU shall set itself the goal "to promote economic and social progress and a high level of employment and to achieve balanced and sustainable development" (Treaty of Amsterdam 1997, 7). The main alteration on this issue, however, was the inclusion of a new title on employment in the treaty: Title VIa which consisted of articles 109n to 109r (The numbering of the articles was later changed to 125-130).

The inclusion of the new title on employment was a recognition of the importance of employment and the fight against unemployment by the EU. The economic policies of the EU that involved the adoption of a number of community-wide rules were meant to facilitate the internal market of the bloc. But these policies also had potential drawbacks since they inhibit or prohibit the independent decision-making of the governments of the member states in some areas. The competition policy of the bloc, for instance, prohibits state aid in article 92 in the section on "aids granted by states" of the Treaty establishing the European Economic Community (2015). The treaty declares

> "any aid, granted by a Member State or granted by means of State

> resources, in any manner whatsoever, which distorts or threatens to distort competition by favouring certain enterprises or certain productions shall, to the extent to which it adversely affects trade between Member States, be deemed to be incompatible with the Common Market." (Treaty establishing the European Economic Community 2015)

The treaty thus deprives individual member states of an important tool that their governments could otherwise use to address economic problems that have the potential to result in increasing unemployment in their country. Another instrument that states could theoretically employ to deal with economic problems in their country is monetary policy, particularly the raising or decreasing of interest rates which might be done to react to economic developments such as recessions, or the overheating of an economy, and the forming of asset bubbles. But this is another area where the EU stripped its member states of an important competence. The formation of the euro required those countries who were joining the euro zone to give up most of their independent monetary policy. Monetary policy in the EU is primarily the competence of the European Central Bank (ECB) and the European System of Central Banks (ESCB).

The Treaty of Amsterdam came into force in the same year when the euro was launched. The inclusion of the title on employment in the treaty is an acknowledgement that the economic and monetary policy of the EU could have a significant effect on employment and member states' ability to address any developments that might affect EU citizens' opportunities for labor in a detrimental way and that some coordination and cooperation on European level is necessary to alleviate any negative effects which the process of economic integration may have on the economies of individual member countries.

Article 109n, the first article on employment that was newly introduced in the EU treaty with the Amsterdam Treaty (1997, 33), therefore declared that the "Member States and the Community shall, in accordance with this Title, work towards developing a coordinated strategy for employment and particularly for promoting a skilled, trained and adaptable workforce and labour markets responsive to economic change." The treaty then goes on to stress the importance of cooperation between member states on the issue of employment. As spelled out in Articles 109o and 109q of the Amsterdam Treaty (1997, 33), policies on employment (and their coordination) were supposed to be consistent with the broad economic guidelines provided by Article 103 (2) of the Treaty on European Union.

In his review of the Amsterdam Treaty Guggenbühl (1997) criticized the new title on employment as insufficient as a foundation for the promotion of employment in the EU. His main point was the Community's lack of significant economic tools that could be used to facilitate employment. In Guggenbühl's (ibid.) view, the reliance of the EU on guidelines and suggestions fell short of achieving any notable outcome in the creation of employment. This also applied to the incentive measures introduced by Article 109r of the Amsterdam Treaty (1997, 33) which Guggenbühl (1997) criticized for being too restrictive in only aiming at sharing methods, knowledge, and strategies across member states without taking concrete steps to increase employment. He also found fault with the overly bureaucratic decision-making procedures in this policy area. Guggenbühl questioned whether the new title on employment would make much of a difference: "The added value of this title is rather dubious if one considers that the EU already made the relevant recommendations to Member States in 1993 by adopting the Delors White Paper on Growth, Competitiveness and Employment." (Guggenbühl 1997, 3) Moravcsik and Nicolaidis (1999, 63) portrayed the inclusion of the new title on employment in the treaty as a "symbolic move." In their estimation the changes brought about by this treaty were neither likely to result in the coordination of financial transfers for the improvement of labor market conditions in any particular member state nor would they facilitate meaningful labor market reforms (ibid.). Janine Goetschy and Philippe Pochet (1997, 608) pointed out that it was only possible to reach a consensus in this policy area because "national policies to promote employment remain[ed] high on the agenda" and since larger programs with comprehensive expenditure were avoided at EU level.

Mark A. Pollack (2000) has argued that the British government of Tony Blair, who had come into office as British prime minister just a few months before the signing of the Treaty of Amsterdam, had a discernible influence on this treaty – so far so that he referred to it as a "Blairite treaty" (Pollack 2000, 266). It could be argued that the promotion of a "skilled, trained and adaptable workforce" and of "labour markets responsive to economic change," as mentioned in Article 109n of the treaty (Amsterdam Treaty 1997, 33), are indeed to some extent in keeping with New Growth Theory, the economic philosophy that was adopted by Blair's New Labour. New Labour tried to chart a new – third – way between the Keynesian economic policies of the post-World War II period and the neoliberal policies of his conservative predecessors John Major and Margret Thatcher (Pollack 2000). New growth theory was focused on the importance of knowledge as a driver of economic growth. Blair's reformed party adopted this view and focused on the facilitation of a skilled labor force and promoted the flexibilization of the labor market. New Labour wanted to initiate a "skills revolution and the creation of a highly trained knowledge-based workforce (education reform with a technology focus)" (Cerny and Evans 1999, 13). The party ultimately ended up more on the neoliberal side of the above spectrum of economic policies. So did some other countries in Europe which modelled their labor market policies after those of Britain. Against this backdrop Bob Jessop (n.d.) warned that "the consolidation of a Blairite neo-liberalism in Britain could become a Trojan Horse through which a transatlantic neo-liberal project penetrates further into the European Union."

The change in British government in 1997 also had a significant effect on the social policy position of the United Kingdom in the EU. The previous government of the United Kingdom under the leadership of prime minister John Major had opted out from the Protocol on Social Policy, also known as the "Social Chapter," that was annexed to the Treaty establishing the European Union. But with New Labour coming to power, the United Kingdom was ready to join the Protocol and also agreed to its incorporation into the body of the EC treaty (European Commission 1997). With its opt-out, Britain had refrained from the implementation of the European Works Councils' Directive and the Directive concerning Parental Leave (ibid.). But this changed with the United Kingdom joining the Social Chapter. These directives became fully applicable in Britain with the Treaty of Amsterdam coming into force on May 1, 1999.

Moreover, the Social Chapter was amended to incorporate additional provisions on positive action for women and an explicit legal foundation for laws pertaining to gender parity in the workplace. Article 119 (later renumbered as Article 141 EC) mandates that each Member State ensures equal pay for male and female workers performing equal work or work of equal value. Pay, under these provisions, is defined as including wages or any form of compensation, either direct or indirect, provided by the employer. Equal pay without discrimination based on sex requires that piece rate pay be calculated by the same unit and that time rate pay be the same for the same job (Treaty of Amsterdam 1997).

Article 119 required the Council, after consulting the relevant committees, to adopt measures to ensure equal opportunities and treatment in employment, including equal pay. It also stated that member states were expected to implement measures to assist the underrepresented sex in pursuing vocational activities (Treaty of Amsterdam 1997). The Treaty of Amsterdam's amendments established a legal foundation for subsequent equal pay laws and gave member states the authority to continue or implement compensatory measures that could help members of underrepresented sexes seek employment or make up for disadvantages in professional careers (Burrows 2010).

Another important issue concerning the political economy of the EU was the incorporation of the Schengen Agreement in the body of the treaties. The Schengen Agreement of 1985 is a treaty centered on the free movement of people across the borders of the member states of the European Community and the four countries of the European Free Trade Association (EFTA), Iceland, Liechtenstein, Norway, and Switzerland. Ireland and the United Kingdom opted out from this agreement. With the incorporation of Schengen in the *acquis communautaire* of the EU, the free movement of people throughout much of the European continent was enshrined in the law of the bloc (Huysmans 2000). The Treaty of Amsterdam also regulated and improved the conditions for the movement of non-EU citizens in the area of the EU (ibid.). With the inclusion of the free movement of people in the text of the treaty, the EU finally reached what was already set as a goal with the Treaty of Rome in 1957 which envisioned this freedom for the whole of the European Economic Community. In Article 3 (1c) the Treaty of Rome set as a goal "the abolition, as between Member States, of the obstacles to the free movement of persons, services and capital" (Treaty establishing the European Economic Community 2015, 5).

Conclusion

The Treaty of Amsterdam aimed to reform the institutional structure and decision-making processes of the EU. The treaty included several protocols, declarations, and amendments to existing treaties. Despite earlier significant changes brought by the Single European Act and the Maastricht Treaty, further adjustments were necessary due to the impending European currency union and the anticipated enlargement of the EU. The Treaty of Amsterdam sought to modernize the EU by increasing the authority of the EP and the European Court of Justice. The EP was given more authority, including the power to approve the nominee for Commission President. The treaty extended the use of QMV to 14 relatively uncontroversial areas, while more sensitive issues remained under unanimity. It also introduced greater flexibility for member countries to cooperate in specific policy areas. The treaty also moved many issues from the third to the first pillar, such as border control, immigration, and refugee protection, applying community rules to these areas. While it allowed closer cooperation among member states, it granted opt-outs to countries like Britain, Ireland, and Denmark. Despite these changes, some scholars viewed the treaty as lacking in substance, particularly due to its failure to address the reweighting of votes in the Council, which was seen as crucial for the accession of Central and Eastern European states. This issue was later resolved in the Treaty of Nice.

The treaty also emphasized cooperation between member states on employment, but it did not address major issues like the independent use of monetary policy, which was centralized under the ECB. However, the treaty's provisions on employment were criticized as insufficient and lacking concrete measures to promote employment. Additionally, the incorporation of the

Schengen Agreement into EU law enshrined the free movement of people within much of Europe, though the United Kingdom and Ireland opted out. Furthermore, the United Kingdom, under Prime Minister Tony Blair, ended its opt-out from the Social Chapter, which led to the implementation of important labor directives, including parental leave and equal pay for men and women, strengthening social policy across the EU. Some scholars of European politics criticized this treaty for missing out on initiating substantive institutional and policy reforms. Given the lack of significant advancements it brought about, this document can be seen as transitional, serving as a bridge between the more significant Treaties of Maastricht and Nice.

Chapter 7

The Nice Treaty and the Integration of the New Member States of Central and Eastern Europe in the European Union

Introduction

When ten new member countries (NMS, EU-10) joined the European Union (EU) on 1 May 2004, they had gone through an excruciating process of scrutiny and reforms which prepared them for the accession to the bloc which comprised 15 member states (EU-15) at the time. Each individual candidate for accession had to meet a set of criteria for accession and of course also agree to the existing body of laws of the EU, in the EU also commonly known by the French term *acquis communautaire*. But it was not only the NMS who had to implement comprehensive reforms, the EU itself also adopted a number of changes that were supposed to ready the bloc for the accession of the new members.

A major step in this direction was taken with the Treaty of Nice which was signed on 26 February 2001 and came into force on 1 February 2003. The Treaty of Nice addressed the need to overhaul the decision-making structure of the bloc and design it in a way that fit the needs of a Union that was about to grow from 15 to 25 members. This included a reform of the weighting of votes assigned to individual member countries for decisions taken by the Council of the European Union. Whereas all countries saw an overall increase of their individual shares in the votes, the reweighting favored the larger members in terms of population such as Germany, France, Italy, and the United Kingdom which was still a member of the bloc at the time. Previously, these countries were clearly disadvantaged in terms of their voting shares. More importantly in this context, the Nice Treaty prepared the bloc for the accession of the eight NMS from Central and Eastern Europe (CEE), the Czech Republic, Estonia, Latvia, Lithuania, Hungary, Poland, Slovenia, and Slovakia, and of the two Mediterranean countries Cyprus and Malta by allocating the voting shares for them. This made sure that the NMS would be able to properly take part in the decision-making procedures of the EU. The Treaty of Nice also included some further changes of the institutional structure of the EU and the extension of *qualified majority voting* (QMV) to several dozen treaty provisions which affected a wide range of specific policy areas. These measures had the purpose of providing the EU with an institutional structure and a procedural framework that allowed for a smooth decision-making process.

This study attempts to determine whether and how far the integration of the NMS in the EU can be considered a success. The criteria on the basis of which this can be decided are the economic development of the NMS after joining the EU as measured by the growth of GDP and of trade flows from and to the NMS. They can also be measured by looking at the participation of the NMS in the monetary transfers of the EU. In this context it will also be interesting to analyze migration flows from the NMS to the old member states (OMS), because of the predictions that were made about developments in this field that might have negative effects on both the NMS as well as the OMS. An assessment of the integration process with an exclusive focus on economic data would be incomplete, which is why this study also includes socio-economic data about developments of employment and demographic data about migration trends.

It is striking that in the literature there are only very few studies that cover the long-term integration process of the NMS. This process has mostly been discussed as a success. Timo Baas and Herbert Brückner (2011), for instance, have highlighted the benefits of EU enlargement for the bloc as a whole, especially in terms of GDP growth, wages, and employment. Daan Freeman et al. (2022) found that EU membership had a positive impact on the trade relations of almost all member states. They emphasized that it was particularly beneficial for the NMS. According to Vladimir Georgescu (2014), the inclusion of the NMS in the trading system of the EU resulted in increasing economic dynamics in these countries as the volume of their overall involvement in international trade increased significantly. The analysis of Jale Tosun (2014) suggests that the NMS were at least for some years more effective in spending European Regional Development Funding than the old member states. There are also clear signs that fears about large migration flows from Eastern to Western Europe in the form of "migration shocks" (D' Auria et al. 2008, 10) due to the accession of the NMS were greatly exaggerated. However, there have also been voices that raised doubts about the successfulness of this process or at least painted a mixed picture. Zhao et al. (2022) came to the conclusion that the integration process has resulted in a heterogenous outcome for different groups of countries in the EU. While the OMS benefitted more from the integration process than the NMS, there have also been some benefits in the CEE, but to a lesser extent and to different degrees. Whereas KucCzarnecka et al. (2021) paint a very negative picture of the impacts of EU enlargement on the NMS. They claim that it was primarily the OMS who benefited from the integration process – at the expense of the NMS who experienced a process of deindustrialization and served as a source of cheap labor for the OMS. Rant et al. (2020) pointed out that problems in the NMS such as democratic backsliding in Hungary and Poland and high levels of corruption in Bulgaria and Romania resulted in a form of enlargement fatigue in the EU. There is no consensus in the literature on the question whether the integration of the NMS in the EU can be considered as a success or as a failure. One of the goals of this paper is to bring more clarity to this debate.

This study shows how the Treaty of Nice provided the organizational framework for the accession of the NMS as a precondition for the later integration of the NMS. The second section of this chapter gives a brief overview over the main changes which the Nice Treaty included. The main focus is on the measures that were meant to prepare the EU for the accession of the NMS from CEE. This is followed by a section that focuses on the involvement of the NMS in EU policy making and their participation in regional funds and agricultural payments. The fourth section analyzes how far the NMS were integrated in the EU economically and socially. It particularly looks at the development of economic growth, employment, trade, and patterns of migration in the years after the accession of the NMS. The study concludes with a summary of the findings and an outlook on the future of the NMS in the EU.

The Main Features of the Treaty of Nice

The leaders of the EU were aware for some time that a comprehensive change to the treaties was necessary to prepare the bloc for the accession of the NMS. The enlargement round of 2004 was the largest so far in terms of new citizens and of new member countries as well. The ten new member states added 75 million new citizens to the EU and increased the overall number of EU citizens to 450 million at the time (European Commission, 2006). Attempts were already made when the Amsterdam Treaty of 1999 was negotiated to include provisions in this treaty that would get the bloc ready for this massive round of new accessions. However, these attempts failed, which left the legal preparation of the enlargement to the Treaty of Nice. For this purpose, the European Council had to convene an Intergovernmental Conference (IGC), which is the institution responsible for the negotiation of any amendment of the treaties. It primarily consists of representatives of the individual member states, the European Commission and to a lesser extend of the European Parliament. The procedure for the convening of the IGC and for the adoption of treaty amendments is regulated in Article 48 of the *Consolidated Version of the Treaty of the European Union* (Official Journal, 2008).

There were three main issues concerning the NMS which the Treaty of Nice had to focus on: This included the composition of the Commission and the allocation of commissioners to each member state, the number of votes allocated to each member state in the Council, as well as the number of seats for each member state in the European Parliament. Since few of the treaty provisions took effect only after the accession of the NMS in May 2004 – the new weighting of votes in the Council took effect from 1 November 2004 and the allocation of seats in the European Parliament applied after the European elections of 10-13 June 2004

– these issues had to be determined preliminary in the accession treaties (European Commission, 2003).

From here on the three main institutional issues concerning the NMS are discussed in more detail. The first concerns the number of commissioners per state. The EU has been working on reducing the number of commissioners per state for quite some time – with limited success. In the lead-up of the Amsterdam Treaty, the ICG debated a reduction of the number of commissioners. At the time, the larger member states had the right to propose a second commissioner, whereas the number of commissioners that could be appointed by the smaller states was limited to one. The compromise formula found by the ICG was a general limitation of the number of commissioners to 20 (as stipulated in article 213 [ex article 157] of the Consolidated Version of the Treaty establishing the European Community), which – in a situation with 15 member states overall – meant that the five largest member states could still propose a second commissioner (Official Journal, 1997). Hence, it was decided that, with the enlargement of the EU to 20 member states and more, the larger member states had to give up that right of an extra commissioner.

The prerogative of a second commissioner for the larger member states was finally terminated with the Treaty of Nice. The plan back then actually was to reduce the number of commissioners below the number of member states. In a press release on the Treaty of Nice the European Commission (2003, 4) described this plan: "As from the first Commission which will be appointed once the Union reaches 27 Member States, there will be fewer Commissioners than there are Member States. The Commissioners will be selected by a system of rotation that will be fair to all countries." However, the reduction of the number of commissioners to a level lower than the number of member states did not take place. Reducing this number obviously is a delicate proposal, because it affects the sense that individual member states have of their proper representation in the European Commission. The Treaty of Nice amended article 213 stating in article 4 of the *Protocol annexed to the Treaty on European Union and to the Treaties Establishing the European Communities*: "The Commission shall include one national of each of the Member States. The number of Members of the Commission may be altered by the Council, acting unanimously." (Official Journal 2001, 52) The European Commission subsequently decided that the number of commissioners per country should remain one for the time being. The task of reducing the number of commissioners was left to the Lisbon Treaty, which was signed in 2007 and came into force in 2009. The Treaty of Lisbon (Official Journal 2007, 20) inserted article 9 D (article 17 of the Treaty on European Union) which stipulates in subparagraph 5 that as of 1 November 2014 the European Commission "shall consist of a number of members [...] corresponding to two thirds of the number of Member States, unless the European Council, acting unanimously, decides to alter this number." But concerns of individual member states about their proper representation in the Commission still weighed strong and prevented this reduction from happening to date. "In 2009, the European Council decided that the Commission would continue to consist of a number of members equal to the number of Member States." (Mussa 2022)

The second important amendment that was made with the Treaty of Nice regarding EU institutions with the view to the accession of the NMS was the reweighting of the voting rights in the Council. Article 3 of Protocol A annexed to the Treaty of Nice provided for a reweighting of the voting rights of the old member states in cases where the Council makes decisions based on a qualified majority vote. Another document annexed to the Treaty of Nice is the *Declaration on the enlargement of the European*

Table 1. Weighted Votes of Members in the Council of the EU

Country	Number of Votes according to the Treaty of Amsterdam	Number of Votes according to the Treaty of Nice	Difference
Germany	10	29	19
United Kingdom	10	29	19
France	10	29	19
Italy	10	29	19
Spain	8	27	19
Poland		27	
Romania		14	
Netherlands	5	13	8
Greece	5	12	7
Czech Republic		12	
Belgium	5	12	7
Hungary		12	
Portugal	5	12	7
Sweden	4	10	6
Bulgaria		10	
Austria	4	10	6
Slovakia		7	
Denmark	3	7	4
Finland	3	7	4
Ireland	3	7	4
Lithuania		7	
Latvia		4	
Slovenia		4	
Estonia		4	
Cyprus		4	
Luxembourg	2	4	2
Malta		3	
Total	87	345	

Source: Official Journal (1997); Official Journal (2001)

Union (Declaration no. 20) which retained the reweighting of votes included in Article 3 of Protocol A, but provided for a further distribution of votes for the potential NMS and indicated exactly how many votes each country would get (Official Journal 2001). Table 1 gives an overview over the weighted votes of the individual member states. It also shows the votes that were allocated to each member country with the Amsterdam Treaty and the changes that were implemented based on the Treaty of Nice.

As indicated in table 1, all old member states gained votes. The larger countries in terms of their population such as Germany, the United Kingdom, France, and Italy gained considerably more votes than smaller countries such as Denmark, Finland, and Luxembourg. It is also noteworthy that the symbolic parity among the larger member states has been kept. Whereas Germany, the United Kingdom, France, and Italy each had 10 weighted votes according to the Treaty of Amsterdam, the reweighting in the Treaty of Nice increased their weighted votes to 29 for each of them.

With the weighting of votes according to the Amsterdam Treaty, the size of the population of the individual member states was only loosely represented in the share of votes that was allocated to these states. One of the two weighted votes for Luxembourg in the Council roughly represented 200,000 citizens, whereas one of the ten weighted votes of Britain represented about 6 million citizens. This could, as the British government had once pointed out, result in the hypothetical situation where a minority of the smaller states had the power to block legislation where qualified majority voting was required (House of Commons 2000). This was an issue that became even more pressing with a large number of smaller states about to join the EU. The reweighting of votes established by the Treaty of Nice addressed this imbalance to some extent. While it did not introduce any form of exact equivalence between population size and weighted votes, it increased the votes of the larger states to an extent that made the scenario of a majority outvoted by a minority in terms of population size virtually impossible.

What constitutes a qualified majority in the Council is regulated by Article 16 (4) of the Consolidated Version of the Treaty on European Union (Official Journal 2012) in combination with Articles 235 and 238 (2) (ex Article 205 (1) and (2), TEC) of the Consolidated Version of the Treaty on the Functioning of the European Union (Official Journal 2016). Article 16 (4) of the Consolidated Version of the Treaty on European Union defines a qualified majority in the Council "as at least 55 % of the members of the Council, comprising at least fifteen of them and representing Member States comprising at least 65 % of the population of the Union" (Official Journal 2012, 24). In rare instances, the conditions for the constitution of a qualified majority can deviate from this definition in Article 16 (4); these particulars are regulated by Article 238 (2) of the Consolidated Version of the Treaty on the Functioning of the European Union which specifies that if a vote is taken "where the Council does not act on a proposal from the Commission or from the High Representative of the Union for Foreign Affairs and Security Policy, the qualified majority shall be defined as at least 72 % of the members of the Council, representing Member States comprising at least 65 % of the population of the Union" (Official Journal 2016, 154). The procedure established by the treaties is also known as the "double majority" rule. This principle of the double majority was introduced by the Treaty of Nice and later refined with the qualified majority-rules of the Treaty of Lisbon. "The Treaty of Nice already distilled the principle of a double majority in the traditional weighted voting system to take into account the importance of the populations." (Edjaharian 2013, 674) Declaration no. 20 annexed to the Treaty of

Table 2. Seats for each Member State in the European Parliament

Country	Number of Seats according to the Treaty of Amsterdam	Number of Seats according to the Treaty of Nice	Difference
Germany	99	99	0
United Kingdom	87	72	-15
France	87	72	-15
Italy	87	72	-15
Spain	64	50	-14
Poland		50	
Romania		33	
Netherlands	31	25	-6
Greece	25	22	-3
Czech Republic		20	
Belgium	25	22	-3
Hungary		20	
Portugal	25	22	-3
Sweden	22	18	-4
Bulgaria		17	
Austria	21	17	-4
Slovakia		13	
Denmark	16	13	-3
Finland	16	13	-3
Ireland	15	12	-3
Lithuania		12	
Latvia		8	
Slovenia		7	
Estonia		6	
Cyprus		6	
Luxembourg	6	6	0
Malta		5	
Total	626	732	

Source: Official Journal (1997); Official Journal (2001)

Nice stipulates that for the constitution of a qualified majority any member state may – in addition to the provisions regarding the particular share of the countries who vote in favor of a proposal – "request verification that the Member States constituting the qualified majority represent at least 62 % of the total population of the Union" (Official Journal, 2001, 81). This was the first time that a direct population-dependent provision was introduced into the treaties in the rules regarding QMV. With the Treaty of Lisbon, the threshold for the population represented by those in favor of a proposal was later raised to 65 % (Edjaharian 2013, 674).

The Treaty of Nice also changed the number of representatives of each member state in the European Parliament. Table 2 gives an overview over the number of seats allocated to each state according to the Treaty of Amsterdam and the Treaty of Nice.

With the Treaty of Nice the overall number of seats in the European Parliament has been increased by 106 seats to a maximum of 732 seats once all the prospective members states – including Romania and Bulgaria who gained membership in 2007 – had joined the EU. With the exception of Germany which retained its 99 seats and Luxembourg which retained its six seats, all other older member countries had to give up some of their seats. The accession of the NMS brought about a significant reduction of seats for some of the larger member states: United Kingdom (-15), France (-15), Italy (-15), Spain (-14). With Poland and Romania there were two countries among the NMS who were allocated larger numbers of seats in the European Parliament, 50 seats for Poland and 33 seats for Romania. As with the weighted votes for the Council, the number of seats does not exactly correspond to the population size of the individual member countries. While population size is an important consideration informing the size of the delegations from each member state, another equally important factor in determining the number of representatives is the need to provide each state with proper (that is, visible) representation in the European Parliament.

There have been several other changes which the Treaty of Nice introduced to the institutions of the EU. The treaty, for instance, extended QMV in the Council to a number of policy areas which previously required unanimity (European Commission 2003). With the changes initiated by the Treaty of Nice, the institutional design of the EU was well-prepared for the accession of the NMS and their integration into the institutional framework of the Union.

EU Policy Involvement and Implementation by the NMS

In this section this study will investigate how far the integration of the NMS reached since the latest rounds of accessions in the years 2004, 2007, and 2013. To determine the level of integration the involvement of the NMS in the policy making of the EU and policy implementation is examined. This especially involves the participation of the NMS in the distribution of the budget of the EU and in particular in regional funds and agricultural payments. The levels of GDP achieved by the NMS after their accession to the EU, the migration movements within the EU from East to West, and intra-EU trade among the different regions of the EU also promise to provide some insights into the level of integration reached by the NMS.

The data provided for these different economic, socio-economic, and demographic developments cover different periods of time. This is partly due to the differences in availability of data for these different aspects of the integration process, partly due to the fact that longer term trends are more interesting when it comes to migration trends than for monetary transfers from the EU. What all the data provided in this study has in common is that it provides the most recent data for all the issues that are covered. Hence, the data allows to get a picture of the current status of the integration process.

We will first look at the participation of the NMS in the budget of the EU. One of the main questions is whether the NMS are net contributors or net recipients of the budget of the EU. This can be determined based on a simple calculation of the contributions which the individual member countries made to the EU minus the payments which they have received. As figure 1 shows, in 2018 all the countries which joined the EU in 2004 and the years after have been net beneficiaries of the budget. Which means that all net contributors were older member countries. This especially concerned the larger countries such as Germany, the United Kingdom, France, and Italy.

Figure 1 also shows that the NMS Poland, Hungary, and Romania were among the largest recipients of EU funds. As net beneficiaries Poland received 11.632 billion euros, Hungary 5.026 billion euros, and Romania 3.035 billion euros (Buchholz 2020). As could be expected, the larger countries of the old EU have been the main net contributors to the EU budget, whereas the net beneficiaries are mainly the NMS.

The regional funds and agricultural payments of the EU take up the largest shares in EU expenditure. Hence, it is worthwhile to examine the participation of the NMS in these funds. Their participation in these funds and payments is an issue of particular interest in this context for two main reasons: 1. Some of the regions in the NMS lag behind in development due to their long experience as centralized command economies, the breakdown of some industries after the end of the Cold War, and the difficulties with the transition from command to market economy. 2. For

Figure 1. Net Contributors and Net Recipients of the EU Budget, 2018

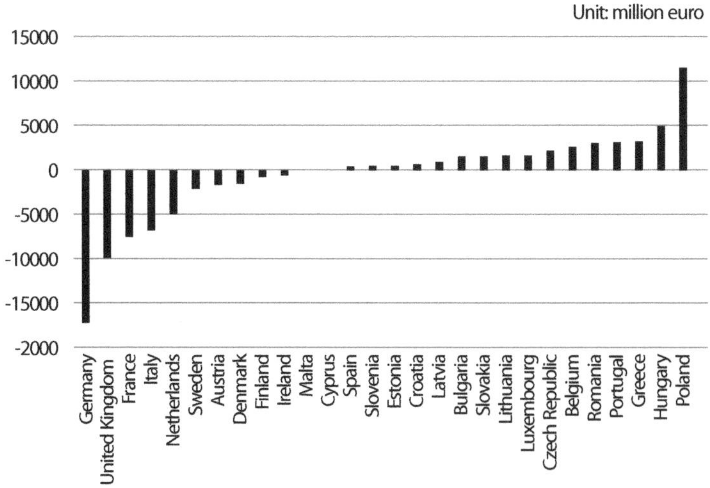

Source: Creation by the author based on data retrieved from Buchholz (2020): https://www.statista.com/chart/18794/net-contributors-to-eu-budget/

some of the NMS agriculture plays a particularly important role, both in terms of the share of the agricultural industry in their GDP and the contribution of the sector to the employment of workers, this especially concerns countries such as Poland, Hungary, Romania, Bulgaria, and Slovakia.

The purpose of the EU's regional funds is to address disparities that exist regarding the level of development reached in particular regions of the EU. There is evidence that the NMS participated very actively in these funds right from the beginning after their accession to the EU in 2004. This does not only concern the amount of payments transferred to the NMS but also the absorption of regional funds by the NMS. The absorption rate was higher in some of the NMS than in a number of old member states. By the end of 2008, the absorption rate of the EU-10 for payments provided by the European Regional Development Fund (ERDF) was as high as 94.37 %, whereas the absorption rate for the old member countries (EU-15) was only as high as 91.03 % (Tosun 2014). This means that the NMS were more efficient in the participation in these EU funds than the old member states. This is a trend which held up in the following years in most of these NMS. As Cristian Incaltarau et al. (2020) have shown, in 2015 the absorption rates of allocated cohesion and structural funds in Poland, Lithuania, Latvia, Estonia, and Slovenia was at roughly 95 %, which means that it was considerably higher than in many of the OMS. In the period of the Multiannual Financial Framework (MFF) between 2007 and 2013, the NMS received cohesion and structural funds that taken together accounted for 21.2 % of their GDP, whereas the regional funds paid to the EU-15 reached 2.2 % of their GDP[1] in the same period (Incaltarau et al. 2020, 944). These figures make it clear that the NMS participated very actively in the European system of regional funds. They were of much higher significance for these NMS as a source of funding and public investment than for the OMS.

In the early years of the European Communities, agricultural payments accounted for the largest share in the budget of the bloc. But that share has continuously decreased over the years. According to the European Commission (2021a), EU spending on the CAP accounted for 65.5 % of the budget in 1985; but it had been reduced to 35 % by 2020. This reduction can partly be explained by the decreasing importance of the agricultural sector in the overall composition of the economies of the EU member states, where a general shift from agriculture and manufacturing toward services has taken place over the years. Another reason for the reduction is, of course, the changes in the CAP and its payment schemes. Guaranteed prices for agricultural products have largely been replaced by direct payments and later decou-

1 GDP measures from 2006 were used as a basis for this comparison.

pled direct payments to European farmers (European Commission 2021b). According to a report of the European Parliament (2015, 11), "one of the most evident results of this process has been the transformation of the CAP from a product-specific policy (the CMOs)[2] to a producer-specific policy."

The NMS have participated in the agricultural support schemes of the EU right from the beginning of their membership. They contributed greatly to the stability of the income of individual farmers and to the sustainability of their livelihoods. Over the last decade farm income has continuously increased throughout the EU. In 2018, the average *farm net value added* (FNVA) was as high as 35,300 euros per farm and 22,500 euros per annual working unit (AWU). However, "significant income differences" have been observed regarding the type of farming and also the particular regions in the EU (European Commission 2021c, 1). The income of farms is the highest in the north-western part of the EU and the lowest in its eastern regions. "The level of agricultural income is generally lower than the average income in the whole economy, but there are variations between Member States." (European Commission 2021d) Between 2005 and 2019, hourly agricultural earnings in the EU have fluctuated between 34.6 % and 50.1 % as a share of the average income in the whole economy (2009 was an exception when agricultural earnings decreased to 32.4% of the average). In the first years after accession, the gap between agricultural earnings and the average income in the whole economy was generally larger in the NMS than in the old member countries (European Commission 2014). This gap has narrowed only in recent years with an overall increase of agricultural earnings in the average income in the NMS.

The MFF of 2014-2020 included another reform for the fi-

---

2 The acronym CMO is standing for Common Market Organization.

nancial support of agriculture. Under this new scheme individual member states had different options of choice for the payment they participated in. As Henke et al. (2015) explained, the most important changes introduced by this reform pertained to the replacement of the Single Payment Scheme (SPS) and Single Area Payment Scheme (SAPS) which constituted the main forms of agricultural payments since the reforms of the CAP in the beginning of the 2000s. "The other components of the direct payments are of a selective nature and oriented to remunerate specific behaviour of farmers (such as in the case of the agricultural practices beneficial to the climate and the environment remunerated by 'green payments') or a specific status (such as being a young farmer or having farms located in areas with natural constraints)." (Henke et al. 2015, 14) A study by Henke et al. (2018) found that OMS and NMS were rather different in the way they made use of the options for agricultural funding provided by the reform. They categorized countries according to the "flexibility, speed and the extent of the transition" (Henke et al. 2018, 409) in their adoption of the changes and found that the NMS were rather reluctant to implement these changes. All the CEE countries who joined the EU in 2004 and 2007 preferred to continue applying the SAPS, whereas the OMS showed differences in the level of the flexibility, speed, and extent to which they adopted the new CAP policies (Henke et al. 2018).

The CAP consists of two main pillars. The first pillar is the European Agricultural Guarantee Fund (EAGF) which includes direct payments for farmers and other measures such as payments for sustainable farming and a special payment program for young farmers (European Commission n.d.-a). The second pillar is the European Agricultural Fund for Rural Development (EAFRD) which aims at the facilitation of the competitiveness of European farmers, focuses on sustainable development, and supports rural economies and communities. Table 3. distinguishes between

Table 3. CAP Expenditure by Member State (2018 and 2019)

Country (OMS)	Total EAGF payments in 2018	Percentage of the EU total	Total EAFRD payments in 2019	Percentage of the EU total
Austria	716,4	1,63	538,1	3,89
Belgium	553,9	1,27	78,9	0,57
Denmark	833,3	1,90	101,1	0,73
Finland	528,4	1,20	351,1	2,58
France	7480,3	17,02	2063,5	14,91
Germany	4910,0	11,17	1273,6	9,20
Greece	2038,7	4,64	411,4	2,97
Ireland	1198,2	2,73	324,0	2,34
Italy	4273,0	9,72	1449,1	10,47
Luxembourg	33,4	0,08	14,4	0,10
Netherlands	703,8	1,60	90,4	0,65
Portugal	775,1	1,76	523,0	3,78
Spain	5690,7	12,96	1165,6	8,42
Sweden	709,2	1,61	226,3	1,64
United Kingdom	3228,7	7,34	773,9	5,59
Subtotal 1	33673,1	76,60	9384,4	67,80
(NMS)				
Bulgaria	805,4	1,83	308,6	2,23
Croatia	288,2	0,66	299,6	2,16
Czech Republic	875,3	1,99	393,8	2,85
Cyprus	55,1	0,13	20,9	0,15
Estonia	134,2	0,31	124,9	0,90
Hungary	1303,0	2,96	511,3	3,69
Latvia	254,0	0,58	206,5	1,49
Lithuania	469,3	1,07	181,2	1,31
Malta	5,7	0,01	19,4	0,14
Poland	3415,6	7,77	1092,2	7,89
Romania	1889,8	4,29	967,0	6,99
Slovakia	456,3	1,04	209,3	1,51
Slovenia	142,1	0,32	120,1	0,87
Subtotal 2	10094,0	22,96 (a)	4454,8	32,19 (a)
Payments to EU	195,3	0,40	0,0	0,00
Total	43962,4	100 (a)	13839,2 (a)	100 (a)

Source: Creation of the author based on data retrieved from the European Parliament (2022)
(a) Due to a rounding effect, the totals and subtotals might slightly deviate from the real sums of the figures and percentage rates provided in this table.

OMS and NMS and gives an overview over the total payments which the EU made to each member state in 2018 in the framework of the EAGF and over the total payments to each member state in 2019 in the framework of the EAFRD. The overall payments made in the framework of pillar 1 were much higher with 43.96 billion euros than the payments for pillar 2 which were as high as 10.09 billion euros. This is mostly due to the fact that pillar 1 includes direct payments, which took up the largest share in these money transfers.

As is shown in table 3, the EAGF payments for the OMS exceeded the payments received by the NMS significantly. The amount of 33.67 billion euros that was paid to the OMS accounted for more than three quarters (76.60 %) of all payments that were made in 2018. This left 10.09 billion euros for the NMS, or 22.96 %. The picture is similar in the area of EAFRD payments. In 2019, the OMS received 9.38 billion euros for rural development which accounted for more than two thirds (67.80 %) of the overall payments in this area, whereas the NMS received 4.45 billion euros, or 32.19 %. These differences can be attributed to the differences in the number of farmers and farms in the OMS and NMS which is much higher in the former than in the latter. Another factor affecting these differences is the size of the farms and the particular agricultural products in the growth and cultivation of which a farm specializes, since some of the payments are coupled to the land area of a farm and to the environmentally sound practice of the farm. A comparison of the structures of farms in the OMS and NMS shows that it is not a uniform phenomenon in neither the OMS nor the NMS. In 2016, the countries with the largest number of farms in the EU were Romania with 3.422 million farms and Poland with 1.411 million farms. But the size of these farms was comparatively small with 3.7 hectares per farm in Romania and 10.2 hectares per farm in Poland (European Parliament 2022). In 2018, Poland and Romania were the largest recipients of EAGF payments (see table 3). But a small farm size is not a general feature of the agricultural industry in the NMS. The farms in three of the NMS, the Czech Republic (130.2 hectares per farm), Estonia (59.6 hectares per farm), and Slovakia (73.6 hectares per farm) were comparatively large – larger than the farms in most of the OMS. Hence, due to the different structures of the agricultural industries, the CAP has to tailor its support for farmers according to the different conditions and needs that exist among farmers in the individual member states.

Economic, Social, and Demographic Developments after the Accession to the EU

The accession of the NMS to the EU had without doubt a strong impact on the economies and societies of these countries. To get a broader picture of this effect, this study will first look at measures of economic growth across the region. It will then look at patterns of employment and developments thereof, the trade relations of these countries within the EU (intra-EU trade) and with non-EU member countries (extra-EU trade). It will furthermore examine immigration movements affecting the NMS. In 2004, the year of the accession of the EU-10, all these countries have seen an increase of their economic growth rate, except for Latvia which maintained the high level of economic growth in 2004 which it had already reached in 2003 with 7.5 % (Johnson 2005). With the exception of Malta, which saw a GDP growth rate of 1 % in 2004, up from 0.2 % in 2003, all NMS had a higher GDP growth rate in 2004 than the OMS (Johnson 2005). Some of the NMS also experienced relatively high inflation rates in 2004. According to Tomas Razauskas and Borisas Melnikas (2009), the relatively high level of inflation in the NMS in the years after accession can partly be attributed to the high growth rates that made more money available and partly to the large amount of infusion of money by the EU, especially through its structural and agricultural funds. In 2006, two years after the accession of the NMS, the European Commission (2006) was enthusiastic about the economic development in these countries: "The 10 new Member States' economies are growing at a rapid pace enabling them to progressively bridge the gap with their richer neighbours." At the same time, the Commission noted that the unemployment rate in most of the NMS was still considerably higher in these countries; with an average of 13.4 % it was 5.5 % above the average of the EU-15. In the first years after accession the GDP per capita of the NMS was considerably lower than in in the OMS. However, in recent years, some of the NMS have managed to catch up with the OMS and have actually superseded some of them in terms of GDP per capita. Table 4 gives an overview of the GDP per capita percentage reached in each country in relation to the average GDP per capita of the EU.

As demonstrated in table 4, until 2021 only one of the EU-10 countries reached a GDP per capita that was higher than the EU average with Malta in 2019 at a rate of 103 %. However, due to the dependency of the small Mediterranean island state on tourism and as an effect of the Covid-19 pandemic, Malta's GDP per capita dropped below the EU average in 2020 (96 %) and 2021 (99 %). In 2021, the GDP per capita of several of the NMS at least came close to the EU average: Czech Republic (91 %), Slovenia (90%), Lithuania (88%), and Estonia (87 %). It is noteworthy that the GDP per capita in Spain (84 %), Portugal (74 %), and Greece (65 %) was considerably lower than in these NMS. This presents a situation where there is still a huge economic disparity between the OMS and NMS – in the period between 2019 and 2021 all the countries with a GDP higher than the average were OMS (with the exception of Malta in 2019). The gap between the OMS and NMS

Figure 2. Employment in the OMS, 2012 and 2021 (population aged 20 to 64)

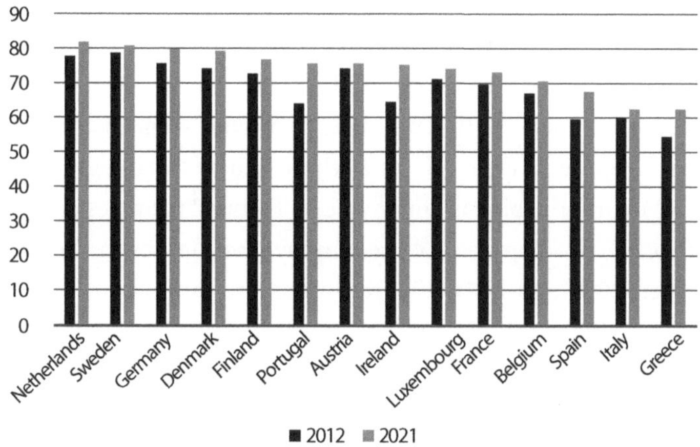

Source: Creation of the author based on data retrieved from Eurostat (2022b)

Figure 3. Employment in the NMS, 2012 and 2021 (population aged 20 to 64)

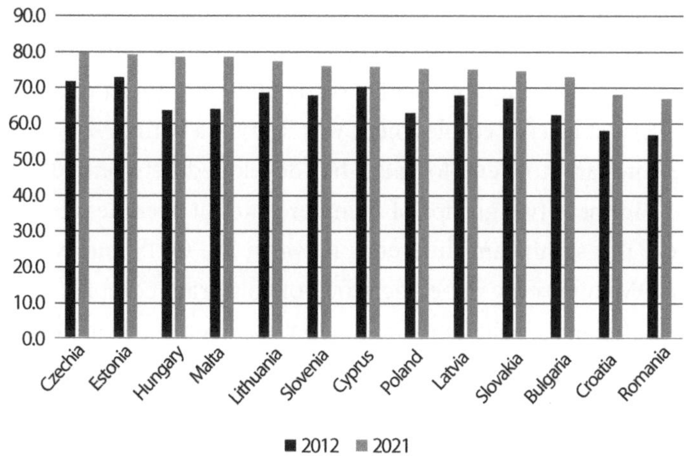

Source: Creation of the author based on data retrieved from Eurostat (2022b)

has not been closed despite of the large monetary transfers of the EU in favor of the NMS. But these percentage rates also show that there is another divide in the EU between the countries of the North-West and the countries of the South.

Another measure that promises to provide some insights into the development of the EU as a whole and of the integration of the NMS into the bloc is employment. Figure 2 provides an overview of the development of the employment figures in the OMS between 2012 and 2021. Figure 3 does the same for the NMS. These two figures show that there has been a general trend of the increase of employment throughout the bloc. Employment rose in this period of time in all member countries without exception. One of the major factors in this development is the increasing labor force participation of women in the member countries of the EU.

In the OMS, the country with the highest level of employment in 2021 was the Netherlands with 81.7 % of the population in the age between 20 and 64 years participating in the labor force. In that year, the OMS with the lowest level of labor market participation of the working-age population was Greece with only 62.6 %. The NMS with the highest level of employment in that age group was the Czech Republic with exactly 80 % and the country with the lowest level of employment was Romania with 67.1 %. When we compare how employment has developed between 2012 and 2021 in these two groups of member states, it becomes clear that there is a significant difference between the OMS and NMS. In the OMS, it is only a specific group of countries, comprising Portugal, Ireland, Spain, and Greece, that has seen larger increases of employment. The main factor in the strong rise of employment is the recovery from the euro crisis, which affected this group of countries severely. The other OMS, on the other hand, have only seen a mild growth of employment, which is partly due to the fact that they already had relatively high levels of employment in 2012. By contrast, all NMS have seen large increases of employment (except for Cyprus where the increase was at an average level). The increases between 2012 and 2021 were particularly high in Hungary and Poland, where employment increased from 63.8 % to 78.8 % (+ 15 %) and 62.9 % to 75.4 % (+ 12.5 %) respectively. Except for Romania, the 2021 employment levels in all NMS who joined the EU in 2004 and after was higher than the EU average of 73.1 %. The strong growth of employment in the NMS and the fact that the employment level in almost all NMS now tops the average of the EU speaks to the positive effect which EU membership had on the economies of these countries and can be taken as an indicator of the successful economic integration of the NMS.

There is, of course, a relationship between the employment figures in the OMS and NMS and the unemployment recorded in these countries. The general increases in employment (figures 2 and 3) have a causal connection to the reduction of unemployment in these states. As shown in figures 4 and 5, the unemployment rate decreased in all EU member countries between 2012 and 2019. In 2020 and 2021, there was a slight increase of unemployment in some countries due to the impacts of the Covid-19 pandemic. The four countries with the highest increases of overall employment, Ireland, Portugal, Greece, and Spain, experienced a significant decrease of unemployment in the period between 2012 and 2021. While unemployment dropped strongly in Greece and Spain for about ten percent in each of these countries, it was still on a comparatively high level with 14.7 % and 14.8 % respectively. Spain was the country with the highest level of unemployment among the OMS (and among all EU member countries as well), whereas Germany recorded the lowest unemployment rate with 3.6 % in 2021. The high levels of unemployment in Greece and Spain can be seen as a long-term effect of the euro crisis and the

Figure 4. Unemployment in the OMS, 2012 and 2021 (population aged 15 to 74)

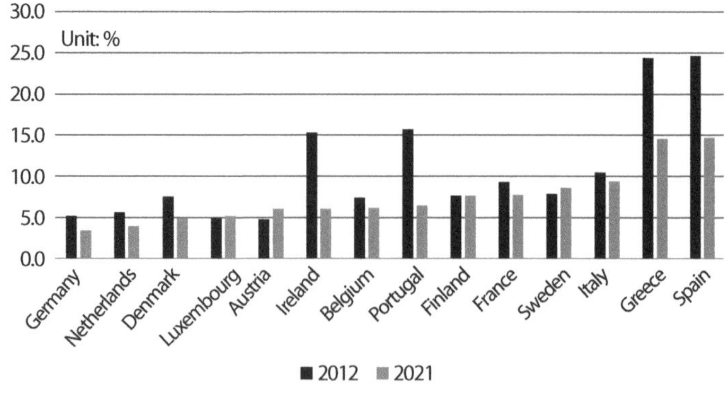

Source: Creation of the author based on data retrieved from Eurostat (2022c)

Figure 5. Unemployment in the NMS, 2012 and 2021 (population aged 15 to 74)

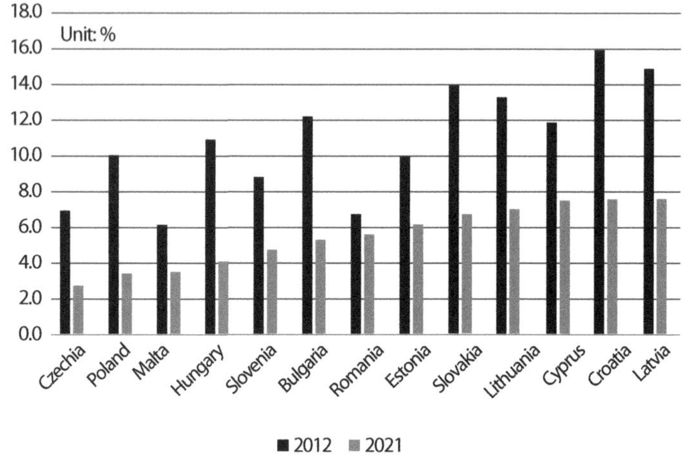

Source: Creation of the author based on data retrieved from Eurostat (2022c)

failed or imperfectly working attempts at crisis mitigation by the EU.

By contrast, the unemployment rates in all NMS, except for Romania, dropped significantly between 2012 and 2021. Latvia and Croatia recorded the highest unemployment rates of the NMS with 7.6 % each. Both countries experienced a considerable reduction of unemployment in the period investigated. In Croatia the unemployment rate was at 16 % in 2012; in Latvia it was at 15 %. In 2021, the lowest unemployment rates were recorded in the Czech Republic and in Poland with 2.8 % and 3.4 % respectively. It is noteworthy that the unemployment rate of the Czech Republic was below the rate of Germany. Moreover, while there still was relatively high unemployment in Croatia and Latvia, it was nowhere near the high levels seen in some of the southern European countries. This is consistent with the insights provided by the rise in employment: It can again be taken as an indicator that the integration process is working for the NMS.

Migration was another matter of concern when ten NMS joined the EU in 2004 and another two followed in 2007. Because of the large economic differences between the OMS and NMS, there were two major worries related to migration: 1. Many citizens from the NMS would seek job and business opportunities in the OMS and unbalance the labor markets there. 2. By leaving their home countries in large numbers they would weaken the economies of these countries and cause a brain drain from the East to the West of Europe. There was a number of studies which estimated that 2 % to 4 % of the population of the NMS would move to the OMS. There were even some estimates that were as high as 7 % to 8 % (Kahanec and Zimmermann 2009). Some authors referred to the influx of about 1 million immigrants from the EU-10 (2.5% of the EU-10 population) to the EU-15 that actually happened in the period between 2004 and 2007 as a "migration shock" (D' Auria et al. 2008, 10).

The fears that mass migration from the NMS could overwhelm the labor markets of the OMS resulted in transitional agreements which, for instance, involved the mandatory registration of labor migrants from the NMS in some of the OMS and also delays in the opening of the labor markets to immigrants from the NMS in few OMS. In 2004, most of the EU-15 moved forward only with a limited opening of their labor markets for citizens of the NMS. The only countries which fully opened their labor markets right from the start were Ireland, Sweden, and the United Kingdom (Breitenfellner et al. 2008). Germany and Austria, for instance, made use of a 7-year period during which their labor market remained closed to immigrants from the NMS. They fully opened their labor markets to workers from the EU-10 only in 2011. However, there also is evidence that the fears of the possible negative effects of the migration flows were largely exaggerated. In fact, the influx of the workers from the NMS had a stimulating impact on the economy of the OMS and via the remittances and the trade links that accrued from the movement also for the NMS. Timo Baas and Herbert Brückner (2011, 48) have stressed that "the interaction between migration and trade may mitigate the potential labour market effects of immigration. Moreover, migration related factors such as remittances have a substantial impact on trade and other capital movements." In the first years after the largest round of accessions in 2004 only slight annual reductions of the working age population in the NMS had to be registered. At the same time, it became clear that this movement of workers from East to West had a stimulating effect on the economies of the OMS who were receiving new workers (D' Auria et al. 2008). This proved to be true even for Germany which received only a relatively small portion of the migrants from the EU-8, the NMS from CEE which had joined in 2004 (Baas and Brückner 2011).

Since the labor markets of the EU-15 opened fully to workers from the EU-10 only in 2011, it is interesting to see how migration flows developed in the decade between 2011 and 2020. Figure 6 illustrates the immigration and emigration flows of the OMS in that period. Based on data retrieved from Eurostat, the European Statistics Agency, it was possible to calculate the net migration for these countries. The same was done for the NMS based on data from Eurostat (see figure 7).

Figure 6 shows that the net migration in almost all OMS has been positive for the period under investigation. There are only two exceptions with Ireland and Portugal, where emigration was slightly higher than immigration. Germany is the country with the largest inflows and outflows. But immigration to Germany considerably exceeds emigration. These large numbers can primarily be attributed to the refugee movement of 2015 and 2016 which is not in any way related to the accession of the NMS. The same is true for the large increases in net migration in most of the other OMS. However, immigration from the NMS accounts for a significant share in the immigration to these countries.

What is of greater significance in our context are the migration movements from and into the NMS, because most of the outflows have resulted in inflows in the OMS. As figure 6 shows, there are several among the NMS with a negative net migration. The negative balance is particularly high for Poland with a net migration of -227,630 and for Romania with the net migration of -424,231. Other countries with a negative net migration are Bulgaria, Croatia, Latvia, Lithuania, and Slovakia. For Bulgaria, the net migration was almost balanced with 260 individuals more leaving the country than coming into it. The data provided by Eurostat (2022e) clearly show that Poland and Romania recorded the largest migration movements of all NMS, which is not surprising since these are the two largest countries in that group in terms of

Figure 6. Net Migration of the OMS, 2011-2020

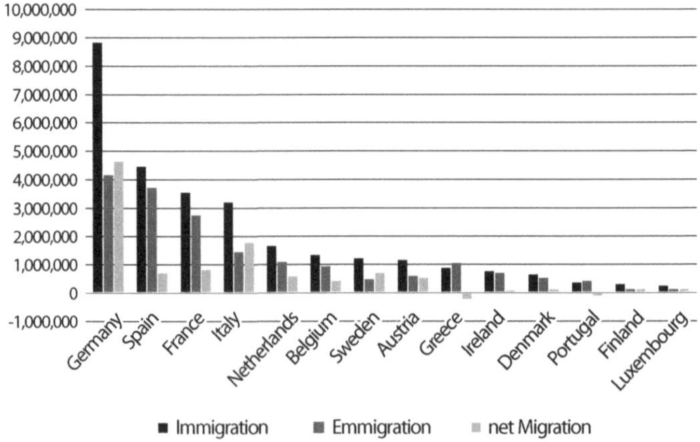

Source: Creation of the author based on data retrieved from Eurostat (2022d)

Figure 7. Net Migration of the NMS, 2011-2020

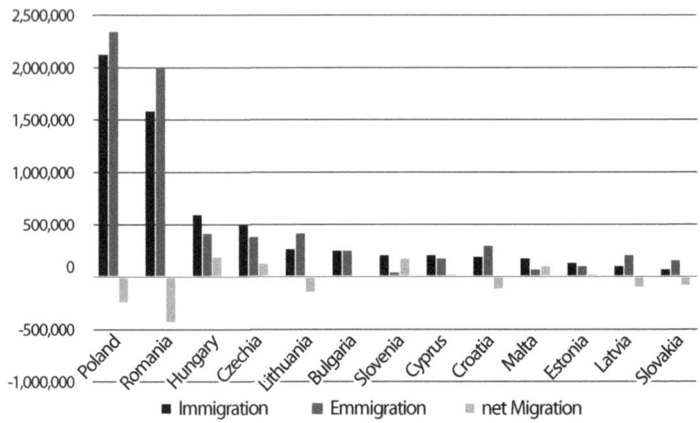

Source: Creation of the author based on data retrieved from Eurostat (2022e)

their population size. While emigration numbers are very high in both of these countries, immigration figures are also large, though not large enough to balance the outflow. Some of the immigrants included in these figures actually are remigrants, that is, returning emigrants – nationals of these countries that return from foreign countries, where they went as labor immigrants or for other reasons at an earlier time.

As data provided by Statistics Poland (2021) show, more than 50 % of the emigrants who left Poland between 2004 and 2020 went to one of the other EU member states. The most significant destination right after the accession of Poland to the EU was the United Kingdom where the number of Polish residents rose to 625,000 between 2004 and 2011. After 2011, the number of Polish immigrants in the United Kingdom increased at a slower pace and peaked in 2016 with 788,000. After 2016, when the British held their Brexit referendum and decided to leave the EU, the number of Polish immigrants in the country decreased. In 2018, for the first time since the accession of Poland to the EU, the number of Polish immigrants in the United Kingdom was lower than their number in Germany. Between 2011 and 2020, Germany became the most important destination for Polish emigrants. The number of Polish residents in Germany rose from 470,000 in 2011 to 706,000 in 2020 (Statistics Poland 2021).

In the early years of Romania's membership in the EU, the main destinations for immigrants from Romania were Italy and Spain. According to a migration profile of the United Nations (n.d.) for Romania from 2013, there were already more than one million immigrants from Romania in Italy and almost 800,000 in Spain. With 383,626 immigrants from Romania, Germany only ranked third among the top destinations for immigrants from that country. However, when Germany opened its borders for nationals from Romania in 2014, the picture changed rapidly. By

2018, almost 60 % of all Romanian emigrants lived in Germany, while their number had strongly decreased in Italy and Spain (OECD 2020).

An area where large impacts of the accession of the NMS to the EU can be expected is trade. With the accession, the conditions under which goods, services, and capital can move across the internal borders of the EU changed strongly. It meant that all tariff barriers and all non-tariff barriers to trade were removed for intra-EU trade. It was to be expected that EU membership would not only change the patterns of intra-EU trade but also of extra-EU trade of the NMS, because EU membership involved these states in the value chains of the EU's export production. It also included them in the many trade agreements which the EU had already entered at the time of accession and the many others which it has concluded since then with non-member countries such as Canada, Japan, and South Korea, and with other trade blocs such as Mercosur (the market of the South composed of Argentina, Brazil, Paraguay, Uruguay, and Venezuela). Intra-EU trade often serves as input for extra-EU trade. In 2015, 53.2 % of the trade in the EU was intra-EU trade (down from 59.6 % in 2005), whereas the share of extra-EU trade was as large as 46.9 % (up from 40.4 % in 2005) (Rodil-Marzába and Campos-Romero 2021). In this same period between 2005 and 2015, the forward participation of intra-EU trade rose from 12.4 to 13.2%. (Rodil-Marzába and Campos-Romero 2021) Hence, the inputs of intra-EU trade into extra-EU trade also increased in this period with the overall increase of extra-EU trade relative to intra-EU trade.

There is much evidence that the inclusion of the NMS in the trade system of the EU resulted in increasing economic dynamics in these countries as the volume of their overall involvement in international trade increased significantly (Georgescu 2014). Similar to the OMS, most of the trade of the NMS is intra-EU trade, whereas the same pattern of decreasing intra-EU trade and increasing extra-EU trade can be observed for the exports from the NMS. However, for few NMS such as Romania the amount of intra-EU imports increased (Georgescu 2014). While there has been a tendency of decreasing intra-EU trade and increasing extra-EU trade, it is important to keep in mind that measured in absolute numbers the volume of the intra-EU trade has actually increased. This was facilitated by the removal of certain barriers to trade, but also by the simple fact that border controls had fallen away when the NMS joined the Schengen Agreement, which in itself resulted in a considerable reduction of costs in international trade (Felbermayr et al. 2018). As Baas and Brückner (2011 48) have documented for the period between 2004 and 2010, Germany's exports to the EU-8 increased by 7 %, whereas the imports from that group of countries to Germany only increased by 3.3 %, which left the country with "a considerable trade surplus." It is clear that the trade of all member countries of the EU benefitted from EU membership. However, it has to be noted that this trade can at times appear asymmetrical, benefitting the countries that are economically, geographically and politically at the center of the bloc more than the countries at the periphery.

Conclusion

This study first gave a detailed overview how the EU prepared itself for the largest accession round in its history so far when ten NMS joined the bloc in 2004 and three others followed with Bulgaria and Romania in 2007 and Croatia in 2013. The Treaty of Nice played a crucial role in that preparation, since it provided for a reform of the EU institutions such as the European Commission, the Council and the European Parliament which made the

EU fit for the accession of the new members and guaranteed that decision-making procedures would run smoothly in the enlarged bloc. It was also found that the accession of the NMS contributed significantly to the economic development of the NMS. While none of these countries has exceeded the average GDP per capita of the EU yet, the GDP per capita developments of the Czech Republic, Estonia, Lithuania, Malta, and Slovenia have come close to this average. Their GDP per capita was higher than that of Greece, Portugal, and Spain.

This was facilitated by the economic boost and the improved conditions regarding trade and foreign direct investment which the membership of the NMS in the EU provided to these countries. The large payments of the EU to the NMS in the framework of the regional and agricultural funds also were a crucial factor in this integration process. Whereas the standard of living has generally increased in the NMS due to their membership in the bloc, there are still considerable regional disparities in the EU not only between the OMS and NMS but also between the North-West and the South of the EU. Therefore, the cohesion funds of the EU should be further increased and concentrated on improving the competitiveness and standards of living in the NMS as well as in the Southern periphery of the bloc.

Chapter 8

The Constitution of Europe and Supranational Democracy

Jürgen Habermas's Vision of the European Union

Introduction

The Treaty of Lisbon was signed on December 13, 2007 and came into force on December 1, 2009. It has so far been the last of the eight Treaties on the European Union (EU) (including the Merger Treaty of 1967). This treaty, also known as the Reform Treaty, amended the previous treaties in several important ways. Most significant was the introduction of a Council President (Article 9B) and of the post of the High Representative of the Union for Foreign Affairs and Security Policy (Article 9E), who is in charge of the European External Action Service (EEAS), which was also created with the Treaty of Lisbon (Article 13a, 3). Another important change brought by this treaty was the introduction of qualified majority voting in the decision-making process of the Council of Ministers (Article 9C, 3) and the empowerment of the European Parliament (Articles 9A, 9B, 9C, 9D). These changes involved considerable moves toward a deeper political integration and a further federalization of the EU. They brought the EU closer to forming a political union, but stopped short of actually establishing a federation. With its unique institutional structure, the EU has been a political novelty right from the beginning and it has kept this quality with this last treaty of the EU. It is now somewhere between a confederation and a federation, since it displays features of both of these political structures.

The Treaty of Lisbon included many of the provisions of the Treaty establishing a Constitution for Europe, also known as the Constitutional Treaty, which was signed by all the 25 member states in 2004 but rejected in two referenda, one in France and one in the Netherlands, in 2005. The approach of the Constitutional Treaty was bolder than that of the Treaty of Lisbon in that it would have made a more decisive step toward the creation of a federal state. It would have replaced the previous treaties, while the Treaty of Lisbon preserved much of these treaties by just amending them.

For the federalists in the EU and for those hoping for impulses that European integration may give for a cosmopolitan agenda, the Treaty of Lisbon fell short of their expectations. Since the 1990s, Jürgen Habermas, the eminent German philosopher, was among those most vocal in support of a European Constitution. He has published several books, articles, and essays, and given many interviews on the topic of European integration. They all revolve around the same topic: How can the process of European integration be designed in order to establish a supranational democracy and provide the project of the EU with the highest possible level of legitimacy. This is a question which, according to Habermas (2001; 2013), is especially pressing due to the loss of power which the individual member states of the EU experienced due to the process of economic globalization. Habermas envisioned European integration as a potential counterweight to the pressures exerted by globalization and to the disempowerment of political actors on the national level.

His theoretical approach is a repudiation of those who want to counter the forces of globalization with a retreat into the nation-state and by resorting to nationalism. It can be described as a *vision* of Europe as an entity that has clearly identifiable cosmopolitan features and which is propped up by processes of transnational interaction between the publics of the individual member states, thus, constituting something that has been missing in Europe so far: a European public sphere. Habermas's ideas for the future of Europe can be described as *visionary*, because they are rather bold and would bring considerable changes to the way the EU is constructed institutionally. But his views are by no means utopian, because one can clearly follow his arguments for how this new formation of the EU could be implemented. There can be no doubt, that Habermas's ideas go far beyond the changes brought by the Treaty of Lisbon. Their implementation would require a new treaty, one which might be seen as most decisive step of the EU toward the formation of a European federation.

In the second section, this chapter provides an overview of Habermas's positions on European integration and his proposals for the establishment of a European constitution. The third section reflects on Habermas's ideas of how a further federalization of Europe can be achieved without creating a federal state and how to provide democratic legitimacy for the political union that he envisioned. The fourth section treats the need to create a European public sphere, which according to Habermas, is a prerequisite for this supranational formation to be democratic. The fifth section shows how Habermas's ideas on European integration are embedded in the broader vision for the coordination of politics on global level, which may eventually result in a domestic politics of the world. The sixth section reflects on the critique that has been advanced by a number of scholars against Habermas's vision of a further federalization of Europe and the creation of a supranational democracy. These critics view Habermas's proposals as out of touch with the realities of globalization and neoliberal capitalism and therefore reject these ideas. The article concludes with an assessment of Habermas's positions and their potential of his proposals of giving a direction to the further process of European integration.

The Need for a European Constitution

With his contributions to the debate on Europe's future, Habermas took the position of the intellectual who gives unsolicited advice regarding a problem which he, from his somewhat distanced position, may see and understand clearer than those involved in the day-to-day political work and policy implementation of the EU. Habermas (2008a) described the intellectual is an actor, who has "the courage to take normative statements and the imagination for inventive perspectives," someone with an "avant-garde flair for relevance." In his writings on the future of the EU he presented himself as a visionary thinker. Visionary thinking moves outside the framework set by Realpolitik. It is not bothered by the circumstances that put obstacles in the way of an immediate feasibility.

Since the 1990s, Habermas regularly intervened in the debates on the status of European integration and the future of the EU. He made important contributions to the discussion about a European constitution and took a clear stand in favor of such a document. This, for instance, is a position that he took in his analysis of Dieter Grimm's (1995) treatment of the question whether Europe needs a constitution. Grimm had rejected the idea of a European constitution, because it would be the basis for a European state whose institutions would, since there is no European people, necessarily act independent from the will of the people, and thus widen the democratic deficit of the EU and raise questions about the legitimacy of the decisions made by those institutions.

Habermas (1995) in his response to Grimm, agreed with the diagnosis that there is a democratic deficit of the EU. But he came to different political conclusions about how to react to this situation. He concurred with Grimm's views of the potential consequences of a European constitution, namely that "the supranational decision processes would become increasingly independent of the still nationally organised opinion- and will-formation processes," but only "so long as a European-networked civil society, a European-wide political public sphere and a common political culture are lacking" (Habermas 1995, p. 304). A European civil society, a common political culture and European-wide public sphere are elements which Habermas deems to be prerequisites for the democratic legitimacy of a more deeply federalized EU. We will later return to Habermas's proposals for how to introduce these elements.

In his critique of Grimm's positions, Habermas (1995, p. 304) pointed out that the democratic deficit – which Grimm feared would deepen with the adoption of a European constitution – already existed and was widening every day, "because the economic and social dynamics even within the existing institutional framework perpetuate the erosion of national powers through European law." In this situation, it would be crucial not to retreat from European integration into a new nationalism or, as Grimm suggested, to continue on the path of cooperation based on the treaties, but instead to advance this process and provide the institutions that are created on that course and their actions with a higher degree of democratic legitimation. In fact, the newly founded and/or federally empowered older institutions themselves could inspire a new form of identity on European level from which they could draw some of their legitimacy. In this argument for a European constitution Habermas clearly relies on older ideas of *constitutional patriotism*. The concept was first used by Dolf Sternberger and later popularized by Habermas (1986), and meant as an antidote against the new nationalism that emerged in Germany in the 1980s. In this form of patriotism individuals form their identity not in allegiance to the nation but to the constitution.

Habermas (1995, p. 305) proposed the targeted generation of democratic citizenship on European level and hoped that a "legally mediated solidarity among strangers" would emerge with it. According to Habermas (1995, p. 305), the crux of the matter lies "in the fact that the forms and procedures of the constitutional state together with the democratic mode of legitimation simultaneously forge a new level of social integration." If this form of solidarity exists primarily among the citizens of the nation-state, then the crucial point would be to raise it to the European level without necessarily giving it up on the national level. The task at hand was "to *converse* the great democratic achievements of the European nation-state, beyond its own limits" (Habermas 2001, p. 6). This, Habermas (2001, p. 6) held, could be achieved by the adoption of a European constitution to which he attributed the "power of symbolic crystallization which only a political act of foundation can give."

In the run-up to the negotiations of the Constitution of Europe among the member states of the EU, Habermas was a strong proponent and had high expectations of this document. It was clear to him that the EU with its decision on the constitution was at a crossroads where the question was to be decided "whether the institutional status quo, an international balancing of national interests, will be defended with a race to the bottom, or whether the European Union should be developed further into a true federation beyond its current status as a league of states" (Habermas 2003a, p. 96). In this context, it is important to note that Habermas, even though he supported turning the EU into a "true federation," did not advocate the creation of a federal state in the sense of the United States of Europe. Rather, he maintained that a further federalization of the EU is possible without transforming it into a state (Habermas 2014). He was concerned that the transformation of the EU into a federal state would involve the generation of a *hierarchy* between the supranational level and the nation-state level with the former assuming a superior position to the latter. What Habermas (2015) had in mind instead was the establishment of a *heterarchical* relationship between these two levels of government which would involve a balanced power relation between the government institutions on the supranational and the nation-state level.

Disappointment with the Treaty of Lisbon

When the Constitutional Treaty, which Habermas had placed high hopes on, was rejected in the referenda in France and in the Netherlands, what was left was the attempt of the member states to save some of the contents of that treaty and inject it into the Treaty of Lisbon. With the Treaty of Lisbon Habermas (2008c, p. 97) connected "the prospect that (as it is called) 'the substance' of the failed draft constitution can at least be converted into simple European law." Thus, there would at least be some institutional reforms and the possibility to regain the ability to act internally (Habermas 2008c). But in Habermas's view, the Treaty of Lisbon fell short of providing solutions for two of the main problems plaguing the EU. "Originally, the constitution was supposed to create the conditions for (a) a change in the previous political mode and

(b) a decision on the final shape of the European Union." (Habermas 2008c, p. 98)

What troubled Habermas strongly was the elite approach of the EU to decision-making with little or no input from the European citizens that has resulted in democratic deficits of the union. According to Habermas (2008c, p. 98), these deficits have their roots in "the essentially intergovernmental and bureaucratic character of the legislation." He pointed out that the consolidation of the elite structures was particularly noticeable in the adherence to decision-making processes that focus on "the mode of negotiation" and "the renunciation of referenda" (Habermas 2008c, p. 99). He was clearly disappointed with the way the Treaty of Lisbon addressed these democratic deficits. Whereas this treaty expanded the competences of the European Parliament, in his view these expansions did not really address these shortcomings of the EU. For Habermas, the essential question was whether the citizens would notice any of these changes, which he took to be unlikely.

> Because as long as the usual spectrum of opinion-forming within the framework of the national publics is not expanded to include relevant topics and as long as the national publics themselves do not open up to one another, the citizens cannot make use of a formally strengthened position of the parliament. (Habermas 2008c, p. 99-100)

Hence, even though the members of the European Parliament experienced a considerable increase of their competences, Habermas did not perceive this growth in competences as a noticeable expansion of democracy in Europe. What was lacking was the engagement of the European citizens in the processes leading up to the decisions that are made in that parliament. Without a civil society that is involved in such processes, democracy in Europe is insufficient and incomplete. Habermas came to the conclusion that Europe has maneuvered itself into a quandary and he did not see how the Treaty of Lisbon could provide a way out of this situation. In his view, the treaty did not only "cement the existing gap between political elites and citizens" but also missed to "pave the way for a political decision on the future shape of Europe" (Habermas 2008c, p. 105). Neither did the treaty make the EU more democratic in the true sense of citizen participation nor did it provide a clear direction for the future development of the EU. Because of these shortcomings, it was evident to Habermas that further steps would have to be gone in the process of European integration, and for this to happen a European constitution or an amendment of the treaties leading in that direction was inevitable.

The Political Constraints of Globalization

Habermas described globalization as a process that is characterized by increasing economic interdependencies which weaken the capacity of the nation-states to exert control and pursue their independent policies. This growing disempowerment has resulted in "legitimation deficits in decision-making processes" as well as in the nation-states' "increasing inability to provide legitimate and effective steering and organizational services" (Habermas 2003a, p. 89-90). In his view, many of the decisions made by national governments have lost democratic legitimacy because they are influenced by "international treaty regimes" which "largely evade democratic control" (Habermas 2014, p. 86). He depicted the global integration of the market as a process that gave rise to the transformation of the international economic system into a "transnational economy" (Habermas 2003a, p. 88). This resulted in the end of embedded capitalism where national economies were constrained by the capabilities of national governments to rein in the market. "States are now embedded in markets, rather than national economies being embedded within state borders." (Habermas 2003a, p. 88)

These changes have especially affected the capacities of national governments to provide social services and thus brought about a weakening of the social state (Habermas 2008c). With the weakening of the social state came the creeping delegitimization of the nation-state and a crisis of democracy which in recent years spawned the rise of populist political forces in Europe and other places of the world.

> As the limits placed on national governments' spheres of action endanger the social state, they also endanger the project whose success until now has been possible only within the nation-state framework: compensating for the socially undesirable effects of capitalism. (Habermas 2003a, p. 88)

In this situation, Europeans are faced with the choice of either abandoning supranational integration and retreating into the nation-state, on the one side, or continuing on their path toward further integration and trying to regain some of the political capabilities on European level which they have lost on national level, on the other side (Habermas 2014). Taking the latter path could lead to a "transnationalization of democracy" and thus justify the project of European integration as one of "democratic self-assertion" (Habermas 2014, p. 86). What was needed in Habermas's view is a repoliticization of the decision-making processes in Europe. He claimed that it was time to give priority to politics over "the logic of the market" (Habermas 2003a, p. 94). If a European federation was to be founded as a democracy the primacy of politics had to be asserted because "markets, unlike political entities, cannot be democratized" (Habermas 2003a, p. 95).

According to Habermas's analysis, nation-states on their

own do not have the ability anymore to have any meaningful influence on global political developments. Therefore, he stated that the time had come, especially for smaller and medium-sized states to form supranational blocs that speak with one voice and thus gain the ability to re-regulate transnational markets in ways that limit the undesirable effects of global capitalism (Habermas 2008c; 2014). He expressed the hope that the "discrepancies between an advanced economic and a retarded political integration could be overcome by the construction of higher-order political agencies, capable of 'catching up' with the pressures of deregulated markets" (Habermas 2001, p. 14). In choosing that path, the EU could serve as a model for other regions in the world which, in turn, could also start to represent their interests commonly on the global stage. What Habermas (2008c, p. 111) envisioned here was the gradual establishment of a "world domestic policy" for which the formation of the EU as a transnational democracy was the decisive initial step.

The Normative Foundations of a European Federation

In the past, one way to justify European integration has been "the straightforward economic argument that unified Europe was the surest path to growth and welfare" (Habermas 2001, p. 7). There can be no doubt that economic integration in Europe up to the euro crisis has resulted in increasing prosperity across the continent. Thus, the EU was capable of justifying the project of an ever-closer union through outcomes. However, Habermas (2001, p. 8) warned, with the growing pressures exerted by globalization that "henceforward economic achievements can at best stabilize the status quo." To achieve political support for advances in European integration that may lead up to the creation of a political union one would have to do more than provide economic benefits. Hence, the goal of a political union would have to have a sense of higher purpose, because "great political innovations […] demand political mobilization for normative goals" (Habermas 2001, p. 8).

A European federation would need a normative foundation. Habermas (2001, p. 21) stressed that European citizens were ideally prepared to provide further European integration with a normative justification since they were already linked together normatively in many different ways. Habermas published an article together with the French philosopher Jacques Derrida, in which they pointed out that Europeans have much in common regarding their values and their attitudes toward capitalism and the market.

> Europeans have a relatively large amount of trust in the organizational and steering capacities of the state, while remaining skeptical toward the achievements of markets. […] They maintain a preference for the welfare state's guarantees of social security and for regulations on the basis of solidarity. (Habermas and Derrida 2003, p. 295)

Indeed, there is a European tradition in support of certain notions of social justice. Habermas (2001, p. 10) pointed to the "political traditions of the workers' movement, the salience of Christian social doctrines and even a certain normative core of social liberalism" which the EU can build on and justify the pursuit of higher levels of distributive justice in a supranational political European entity. In fact, Habermas suggests that the European welfare state can only be saved through a flight forward, that is, further European integration and the reclaim of the ability to act by European institutions – an ability that has been all but lost by national institutions. For Habermas, the retreat into the nation-state is not a viable alternative due to the forces of globalization that have weakened the capabilities of national governments to pursue their national interests on the international stage.

That there is more to European integration than the promise of economic prosperity, is what the EU Charter of Basic Rights has shown. According to Habermas (2001, p. 21), the Charter articulates a "social vision of the European project." In defining a broad range of freedoms and rights that are protected, this convention is a strong expression of the European commitment to human rights. It is also strong proof of the fact that "Europeans link together normatively" (Habermas 2001, p. 21). Taken together there is much evidence that the EU is much more than an economic bloc or a market. There is "a certain legacy of social norms" (Habermas 2001, p. 10) which European citizens have in common and which they can build on when advancing their project of founding a European federation.

Toward a Political Union Through Policy Integration

To achieve the goal of establishing a political union, several policy areas would have to be integrated which have to date largely been the responsibility of the individual member states of the EU. Habermas (2015) was concerned about the imbalance that was created in the EU as a result of the measures taken against the euro crisis which benefitted the executive branch in terms of institutional power relations at the expense of national parliaments; and even though the European Parliament was involved in most of the decisions that were made to counter the crisis, it did not gain new competences to the same extent other institutions such as the Commission or the Council acquired such (to a large extent informal) competences. In Habermas's view, the situation was exacerbated by the economic disparities that emerged in Europe; and he concluded that "the continuing trend towards growing imbalances between the national economies can be halted in the long run only within the framework of a Union with a common fiscal, economic and social policy" (Habermas 2015, p. 551). For this to happen a further shift of sovereignty from the national to the supranational level would be inevitable.

Integration in the field of fiscal, economic, and social policy is what Emmanuel Macron and Sigmar Gabriel, when they were economic ministers of France and Germany respectively, had already advocated (Habermas, Gabriel, and Macron 2017); but they failed to implement any significant changes back then. Movement in the direction of a common fiscal and social policy has been achieved only recently as part of the measures which the EU has taken against the coronavirus pandemic. Achieving any progress in this field is difficult because it would inevitably involve monetary transfers between individual member countries. For this to be accepted by a vast majority of the European citizens, these very citizens would have to recognize individuals, who are from other EU member countries, as members of the same European political community (Habermas 2003b). It would require a shift in their identity. "The population must so to speak 'build up' their national identities, and add to them a European dimension." (Habermas and Derrida 2003, p. 293) This strengthening of a European identity was deemed necessary so as to "halt outvoted minorities from the obstruction" of the will of the majority (Habermas and Derrida 2003, p. 293).

Habermas also advocated a shift toward a common foreign policy of the EU. He claimed that this was necessary, because the individual member states on their own would not have enough weight to be heard internationally. This is why Europe would have to learn how to speak with one voice. Otherwise, Europe would run the danger not to be heard at all in the future (Habermas et al. 2011). After the Iraq war of 2003, which the Bush administration had started based on false "intelligence" information about a chemical weapons program of the regime of Saddam Hussein,

Habermas (2008a) claimed that it was time for the EU to break away from the dependence on the American ally in the area of defense and security policy. This is why the EU would need its own independent military forces. Finally, a common European foreign and security policy would provide the EU with a higher degree of independence from the US and also allow the EU to bring "a stronger influence of its own to bear on NATO operations and UN decisions" (Habermas 2001, p. 7).

The Institutional Setting of a Federation of Nation-states

The policy integration on European level as suggested by Habermas would be possible only with a reform of the institutions of the EU. This reform would involve a shift of power from the nation-state to the European level and a new power arrangement among those institutions. It would require the creation of new institutions or the transformation of existing institutions into new ones. Habermas (2001), for instance, entertained the idea of establishing a second chamber in addition to the European Parliament. He suggested that the European Council could be integrated into the Council of Ministers and transformed into that second chamber (Habermas 2015). He conceptualized this second house as "chamber of nations" (Habermas 2001, p. 22), a chamber that would have much in common with the American Senate. The parliament with its two chambers would "resemble the Congress in some respects" (Habermas 2001, p. 22). In his comparison of the projected institutions of the EU and existing ones of the US, he stated that the Commission would have to be "less powerful than the White House," but the European Court of Justice be "as influential as the Supreme Court" (Habermas 2001, p. 22).

The competences of the European Parliament would generally have to be expanded to cover all policy fields. It would "gain the right to take legislative initiatives" (Habermas 2015, p. 555) and have some oversight powers over the government. In this institutional framework the Commission would be "*answerable equally*" to both chambers of the parliament (Habermas 2015, p. 555). This would, in Habermas view, increase the democratic legitimacy of the law-making process. "The democratic will of the two constitution-framing subjects would be reflected both in the symmetrical participation of the two 'chambers' in the legislative process and in the symmetrical status of Parliament and Council" (Habermas 2015, p. 555).

For this parliament to function properly, common candidates and lists would have to run in European elections. Parties would have to adopt a European agenda and the reduced focus on national interests be "balanced through a generalization of interests across national borders" (Habermas 2014, p. 94). These developments would be accompanied by the common establishment of parliamentary groups by these European parties, which would eventually result in the establishment of a "European party system" (Habermas 2014, p. 94). Furthermore, Habermas suggested that the relationships between the federal legislature and the national parliaments should be strengthened. In addition, he advocated the reanimation of "the horizontal debate between national parliaments" which may "prompt a re-parlamentarization of European politics" (Habermas 2001, p. 24).

With this governmental structure, the EU would "assume at least some qualities of a state" (Habermas 2001, p. 15), but it would still not become a federal state that would conform to the federal model. Habermas (2001, p. 15) conceptualized it as "federation of nation states" where both levels of government – the European and the nation-state level – have a co-equal, or *heterarchical*, status. This federation of nation-states itself would not turn into a state but retain its character as supranational entity and as such attain a unique character. It could be categorized as state system that neither constitutes a confederation nor a full-fledged federal state, but something between these two classes of state systems.

A "Europe of different speeds"

To some observers the process of European integration appears to have stalled and to be stuck halfway on its path toward a political union. Habermas (2008a, p. 87) attributed this deceleration of the process to the mode of movement which the EU chose for its path forward which he refers to as "convoy model, in which the slowest one sets the pace." He suggested that the EU should depart from this approach and rather focus on going forward with a "Europe of different speeds" (Habermas 2001, p. 23). This would involve "the internal differentiation into a politically more closely co-operating Euro-Union (keyword: core Europe) and a periphery of waiting countries to which accession is open" (Habermas 2016, p. 42). Habermas (2001, p. 25) advocated a "Europe of two or three different speeds" because to him it was "preferable to one that breaks up or crumbles away." Habermas clearly sees the danger that the process of integration could be reversed if it does not move forward with the right pace.

In his analysis of the European integration process, he came to the conclusion that two main movements in this process, deepening integration, on the one side, and enlargement, on the other side gained an increasing tendency to hamper each other, the further they went. "But the deeper the integration reaches and the more the core itself becomes dependent on the periphery, the less harmonious the opposing tendencies of expansion and deepening complement each other." (Habermas 2008c, p. 104) He, therefore, favored a model where different groups of countries continue on their paths with different speeds. First, there is the "core" which moves fast toward a political union, and then there is the "periphery" which moves much slower, because it is more skeptical of European integration.

This is an interesting political interpretation of the conceptual pair core and periphery. Here core and periphery are clearly understood as political terms that denote groups of countries according to their willingness to move forward with the process of European integration. In the context of the euro crisis, these terms were often used partly in a geographical and partly in an economic sense (Havertz 2014). As countries which he considers as a potential part of the core he refers to the countries of the euro zone. The countries which did not join the common currency are clearly more skeptical about integration and less likely to agree on further steps to deepen the union. Thus, he considers them as potential part of the periphery.

Those who are ready to deepen the Union are seen as the core, and those who are in favor of a slower pace of integration are referred to as the periphery. Habermas (2014), for example, mentioned Great Britain and Turkey as possible parts of the periphery. (That was before Brexit.) It is not clear though, whether he considered them as part of a second or a third tier of European integration. It is also noteworthy in this context that Habermas did not always use the conceptual pair core and periphery in a political sense. He, for instance, said that "in retrospect, it is correct that the expansion of the EU to the south (to include Greece, Spain and Portugal) and later to the east took place in the interests of both the core and the periphery" (Habermas 2008c, p. 104). Here he used these terms more in a geographical and economic sense.

Adopting the concept of a "Europe of different speeds" would allow for a "graded integration" (Habermas 2008c, p. 105)[1]

1 In this context, Habermas resorted to the term "graded integration" which was used by Georg Vobruba, who due the complexities of the integration process, resulting from an expansion of the EU, suggested to give up "the idea of a uniform integration in favor of a graded integration" (Vobruba as cited in Habermas 2008c, 105).

of the EU, with some parts of the union reaching fairly high levels of integration and others staying behind or catching up at a speed of their discretion. Habermas has repeatedly stressed that those countries who choose a slower pace should at any time have the chance to catch up with those states who decided to move ahead (Habermas 2008a; 2016). On closer consideration, a Europe of different speeds already exists with the EU, on the one side, and countries such as Switzerland, Norway, Iceland, Lichtenstein, on the other side. The connection of these countries with the EU via association agreements can certainly be seen as an element of European integration, even though not within the union. But the way Habermas uses the term "graded integration" clearly refers to the countries already inside the union.

He also expressed the hope that moving forward with integration in different speeds may allow "to settle the thorny problem of which countries will finally belong to, and which are to be excluded from, the Union" (Habermas 2001, p. 23). Thus, a "Europe of different speeds" could bring more clarity to the process of European integration, since it would force countries and their governments to make a decision on where they are standing regarding the project of the EU.

The Democratic Legitimacy of the Political Union

In Habermas's view the process of European unification had reached a dead end because of the lack of the participation of the population in this process. He criticized that it was carried out over the heads of the population with little, if any, input from the European citizens (Habermas 2011). The problem, in his perspective was, that there was no European civil society that would provide the arena for any debate about European politics among the citizens of Europe. Hauke Brunkhorst (2016) observed that such debate was actually not wanted by those in a position of power in the EU. He claimed that these actors would rather continue with the established administrative mode. "The success of this post-democratic model of government consists in *invisibilizing* all structural, social conflicts and political decisions in the institutional system of the EU. Political decisions become decisions without politics." (Brunkhorst 2016, p. 73) According to Brunkhorst (2016), the whole institutional system of the EU is designed so as to avoid conflict and rather facilitate consensus, and thus, make sure that the European citizens do not become a disturbing factor in the administrative procedures of the EU.

Habermas made several suggestions for how to ensure a stronger participation of the European citizens in the political processes of the EU and thought about how to provide democratic legitimacy for the political union. In doing so he first looked at the sources of legitimacy and diagnosed the current status of legitimacy for the governmental activities of the EU.

> At present, legitimacy flows more or less through the channels of democratic institutions and procedures within each nation-state. This level of legitimation is appropriate for inter-governmental negotiations and treaties. But it falls short of what is needed for the kind of supranational and transnational decision-making that has long since developed within the institutional framework of the Union and its huge network of committees. (Habermas 2001, p. 14)

Habermas concluded that the level of legitimacy provided in the EU was insufficient for the decision-making by supranational and transnational actors. It would not just have to flow from the nation-state level, it had to flow from the European level, too.

Here the question arose how to provide legitimacy on European level, if there were no European people, that is, no European sovereign, who could be the source of this legitimacy. But Habermas offered a solution for this problem: "For a supranational democracy that is still anchored in nation states, we do not need a European people, but individuals who have learned that they are both citizens of nation-states and European citizens in one person." (Habermas 2014, p. 94) He suggested that a "*double sovereign*" was possible: "The constituting authority is to be composed of the entire citizenry of Europe, on the one hand, and of the different peoples of the participating nation states, on the other." (Habermas 2015, p. 554) This would allow the two major actors to balance their interests even before the constitution is adopted. It would also make it possible to codify the *heterarchical* relation between nation-state level and European level in the constitution of Europe (Habermas 2015).

This understanding of sovereignty deviates from the traditional notion of sovereignty, which is since Jean-Jacques Rousseau's (1968) "Social Contract" rooted in the assumed ability of "the people" of a country to form a "volonté générale" (a general will). The process of will formation by a double sovereign would without doubt be more complicated and provide more possibilities for disagreements. It is, in Habermas's view, therefore crucial that each side of this double sovereign acknowledges the other side as holder of equal rights. "The democratic constitutional state guarantees equal treatment in the sense of citizens' equal opportunity to make use of their rights." (Habermas 2003a, p. 87) This principle would now have to be expanded throughout the whole of the EU without giving it up on nation-state level.

This operation would involve for each citizen of the EU giving up some of his/her sovereignty on nation-state level to the benefit of the increase in sovereignty on the European side. The gain of sovereignty on European level would have to be equivalent to the loss of sovereignty on the nation-state side. If this type of equivalence is provided and laid down in the constitution, it should not be too difficult for European citizens to agree on this shift of sovereignty, because their loss as citizens of nation-states is their gain as citizens of Europe. There are, of course, matters of identity that could get in the way of such an equation to work out, this particularly concerns any type of nationalism. Citizens of individual member countries may view their citizenship as more valuable than the citizenship of those from other member countries. This is the reason why Habermas stressed the importance of constitutional patriotism which propagates allegiance to the constitution and its principles, not to the nation in an ethno-nationalist sense.

The peculiar thing with Habermas's "double sovereign" as source of legitimacy for a European constitution is that this sovereign would constitute itself as constituent authority in the same moment in which it adopts its constitution (Habermas 2015). Which means that adopting a European constitution would be "a political act of foundation" (Habermas 2001, p. 6) in a double sense: It would provide the legal foundation for the establishment of a supranational democracy on European level; and it would constitute European citizenship and put it on an equal footing with the remaining citizenship of each European citizen in their individual nation-states. If sovereignty can be expanded beyond the nation-state, as Habermas suggests in his concept of the double sovereign, to the European level (that is, regional level), then there is no reason why it should not be possible to extend it further to the world level and thus constitute a system of multi-level sovereignty. We will get back to this thought in the section on Habermas's considerations beyond Europe.

The Creation of a European Public Sphere

In his work *The Structural Transformation of the Public Sphere*, which Habermas (1989) first published in German in 1962, he examined the structural changes of public discourses over the centuries, starting with the 17th century, and the ways in which they contributed to a particular process of self-understanding of an emerging bourgeois society. With an eye toward European integration, he suggested that there was a need for a renewed round of such transformations. According to Habermas (2008c), a prerequisite for the formation of a supranational democracy on European level is the creation of a *European public sphere*. This public sphere again would be a precondition for the establishment of a common European identity. The prospects for this identity to emerge would even increase "the more the dense fabric of the respective culture opens up inside the individual states for the inclusion of citizens of other ethnic and religious origins" (Habermas 2008b, p. 93). This statement shows that Habermas's considerations about European citizenship and identity are deeply embedded in his cosmopolitan worldviews which involve the principled acceptance of *the other*. "The acknowledgement of differences – the reciprocal acknowledgement of the Other in his otherness – can also become a feature of a common identity." (Habermas and Derrida 2003, p. 294) A specific form of solidarity among Europeans that is akin to the solidarity of the citizens within a nation-state can only emerge if this acceptance of the other is provided. This kind of civic solidarity among Europeans can only be generated, if Europeans from different member states know more about each other; and to achieve that, the public spheres of the individual member states – which to date exist only on this nation-state level – would have to open themselves to each other (Habermas 2008c).

Habermas (2001, p. 17) imagined a European public sphere

as "a network that gives citizens of all member states an equal opportunity to take part in an encompassing process of focused political communication." This would mean a re-politicization of the process of European integration. With a European public sphere in place, European citizens could identify issues of common concern and communicate about them. It would "allow the general public to relate, at the same time, to the same topics by taking an affirmative or negative stand on news and opinions" (Habermas's 2001, p. 18). For this European public sphere to appear it would not be necessary to build a completely new infrastructure on that level. In Habermas's (2015, p. 553) view, "the already existing infrastructure of the existing national public spheres is sufficient for Europe-wide communication. [...] And the existing national media are sufficient, too, provided that they perform a complex task of translation." When Habermas (2015, p. 553) talks about translation, he does not necessarily mean the translation of reports from one European language to another, he rather stresses the importance that the national media of the individual member countries "learn to report also on the discussions being conducted" in the other member countries "about the issues of common concern to all citizens of the Union." This opening of the national public spheres to each other may result in a "transnationalization" (Habermas 2008c, p. 108) of these spheres and finally in the emergence of a new, European, sphere. With the creation of this public sphere, European citizens would be enabled to recognize common and "parallel interests," which again would "give rise to cross-boundary networks and a properly European party system" (Habermas 2001, p. 17). It would also increase the democratic accountability of office holders in the framework of the EU, because an open debate in a European public sphere would force them "to face the fight for the public opinion and to stand up for their cause" (Brunkhorst 2016, p. 70), which they do not really have to bother themselves with in the current situation. As a supranational federation, Europe would be truly democratic only if they stand the test of the debate in the general public of the EU.

Beyond Europe: Toward A Domestic Politics of the World

Habermas's ideas on European integration are embedded in a broader vision for the coordination of politics on global level, which may eventually result in a domestic politics of the world. He saw a federalized EU as "point of departure for the development of a transnational network of regimes that together could pursue a world domestic policy, even in the absence of a world government" (Habermas 2003a, p. 96). He suggested that an EU with a constitution could "serve as a model for forms of 'governance beyond the nation-state'" (Habermas 2003b, p. 805). Habermas envisioned a world where a limited number of global players work together on world level and coordinate their policies on all "distribution-related issues" such as "global energy and environmental issues" as well as "financial and economic policy" (Habermas 2008c, p. 120-121).

For this to become reality new organizations would have to be created and new international laws be enacted. In Habermas's view, the United Nations (UN) are ill-equipped to pursue such an agenda. The UN should rather focus on "the tasks of international peacekeeping and the global safeguarding of elementary human rights more effectively and less selectively than before" (Habermas 2008c, p. 120). At the same time, the world organization should be freed from responsibilities that go beyond these core tasks. A "transnational negotiating body" would have to be created that is sufficiently representative and capable of taking on these tasks

(Habermas 2008c, p. 114). Habermas was aware that these visionary statements could be regarded as unrealistic and speculative, and his theory on supranational "governance beyond the nation-state" (Habermas 2003b, p. 805) be seen as an exercise for the sake of itself (Habermas 2008c). But he maintained that the risks of economic globalization could only be contained through transnational cooperation, the first step of which might be gone in Europe with the rest of the world following. If regional integration of the kind which Habermas suggested were possible in Europe, there is indeed no reason to assume that this should not be possible elsewhere and that this cannot be performed on a global scale.

Critical Responses to Habermas

This section reflects on the critique that was broad forward by other scholars against Habermas's vision of a further federalization of Europe and the creation of a supranational democracy or transnational democracy on European level. The critical views on Habermas's proposals are so comprehensive that they could fill books; and they have been advanced from different perspectives and focus on distinct aspects and nuances of Habermas's proposals. The initiation of a debate about the future of the EU can clearly be seen as an achievement of Habermas.

It is not the place here to give a detailed account of all the works that reacted to Habermas's ideas on the further development of the EU. Rather, this study will in this section concentrate only on the critique advanced against some of the central views voiced by Habermas; and it does not claim to give a full picture of the critical reactions to Habermas's vision of the European future. Some of Habermas's critics came to very different understandings of his positions. There are those who viewed his ideas as a threat to the European nation-state (Auer 2010) and others who criticized them as a defense of that very nation-state (Perju 2018). Some authors focused on the need for ethical closure of nation-states (Parker 2009; Perju 2018), if the heterarchical structure in the relation between nation-states and a federalized Europe as advocated by Habermas is to be based on the ethical achievements of the nation-state. It was also questioned whether this heterarchy is actually achievable and suggested that it was inevitable that what would emerge instead, if Habermas's ideas become reality, is a hierarchical relationship (Perju 2018). Another important issue that was raised is that the expectations which Habermas had regarding what could be achieved with a further federalization of the EU, namely, the taming of capitalism and the protection of the European social state, were exaggerated or even unrealistic (Müller-Doohm 2009; Scharpf 2015; Streeck 2014). The following will treat these particular aspects of the critique advanced against Habermas's ideas.

For Stefan Auer (2010, p. 1164), the proposals by Habermas "to move towards a more federalist Europe" and his ideal of a post-national form of citizenship are "both unrealistic and undesirable," because, in his view, they are based on a flawed assessment of the importance which nationalism and national sovereignty have for the citizens of the individual members states of the EU. Auer also criticized Habermas's conceptualization of European citizenship based on constitutional patriotism which may complement the attachments of individual citizens to their nation-states. He refuted Habermas's claim that Europeans had learned their lesson due to the destructive consequences of nationalism in the first half of the 20th century. Especially with a view to the countries of Eastern Europe who had just recently gained their independence he stated that this idea "may make sense in the particular context of German history, but is far less persuasive for other European nations" (Auer 2010, p. 1173). Auer (2010, p. 1179) discounted Habermas's vision for Europe as a "post-national, post-political, consensual paradise." Whereas Auer's reading of this vision as favoring a post-nationalist EU is correct, it is difficult to see how Habermas's approach to European integration could be characterized as "post-political." The contrary is the case. Habermas (2014, p. 87) repeatedly criticized the consensus-based intergovernmental decision-making favored by European officials and even called to "relinquish intergovernmentalism." He has often stated that this administrative mode has to be changed, and key to this change would be the emergence of a *European public sphere* (which Auer simply ignored in his rendition of Habermas ideas) and a vibrant transnational debate among European citizens about the key issues of European politics. Hence, what Habermas advocated was a re-politicization of the processes of decision-making in the EU – not something that could in any way be called "post-political."

Vito Breda (2006) likewise rejected Habermas's idea of constitutional patriotism as a foundation of social integration in Europe. He voiced concern that solely basing social integration on this sort of patriotism could result in the rejection of "the political claims proposed by Member States that want to protect their national interests" (Breda 2006, p. 335). The aprioristic exclusion of such claims from the political arena, Breda (2006, p. 335) asserted, would endanger "the internal coherence of his [Habermas's] theory of an open communicative democracy."

Etienne Balibar (2012) raised doubt whether it was possible "to bring democracy in the European construction without a 'jump' or 'step aside' from the structures and procedures that were designed to exclude it." He was particularly skeptical that a European *demos* – a demos that does not exist yet and which Habermas hoped would arise from the changes of European institution that he proposed and from the creation of a European public sphere – could be spawned by the implementation of Habermas's approach, which, according to Balibar (2012, p. 10), merely focuses on a correction of the "powerful processes of 'de-democratisation' [that] are at work in our society." But what would actually matter is to counteract these processes with "'material' democratic inventions" that are clearly opposed to them (Balibar 2012, p. 10). Balibar (2012, p. 10) did not see how Habermas's approach could mobilize such counteraction. To him this "overly formalistic conception" of democracy did not have the potential to encourage the emergence of the opposition or movement that is necessary to democratize the EU.

Stefan Müller-Doohm (2009) questioned the viability of Habermas's suggestion that capitalism could be tamed and re-regulated through a further democratization of Europe.

> Habermas never tires of demanding that the economy be tamed by democracy. But for the time being it leaves open which political programs and state initiatives are required in a decentralized global society that take democratic legitimation criteria into account. (Müller-Doohm 2009, p. 513)

Müller-Doohm also raised the possibility that Habermas's expectations regarding the impact which the introduction of democratic procedures into the management of the capitalist economy may have could be too high. In Müller-Doohm's (2009, p. 513) view, "the mechanisms of participation and deliberation" could be easily "overwhelmed with filling the functional gaps in the markets." He worried that Habermas's program of "domesticating capitalism" could eventually end up in inadvertently stabilizing and supporting that very system and its excesses (Müller-Doohm 2009, p. 514). Owen Parker (2009, p. 401) pointed to the "competitiveness agenda" which the EU has pursued for a long time and the "neo-liberal rationalities" associated with this agenda. In his assessment, this agenda conflicts with the "norms such as social solidarity," as promoted by Habermas (Parker 2009, p. 401). It is therefore questionable whether the EU will be in a position to rein in capitalism even if the process of European integration progresses and results in increased policy coordination on European level. In this context, Fritz W. Scharpf (2015, p. 12) noted that "not all problems resulting from globalization require European solutions" and that some of these problems themselves were actually brought about by European integration. He added that even where there are European solutions, the question remains how to provide democratic legitimacy for these.

Lawrence Wilde (2007) generally questioned Habermas's conceptualization of civic solidarity as a result of constitutional patriotism and in opposition to national solidarity:

> It seems that Habermas is setting an impossible task in seeking to 'expand' civic solidarity to the European sphere, because that form of solidarity is bound up with national consciousness too closely to permit the conceptual distinction that is so important to him. (Wilde 2007, p. 59)

Which is why he comes to the conclusion that "Habermas's conceptual distinction between national consciousness and civic solidarity simply does not work." (Wilde 2007, p. 60) What added to his doubts was that "solidarity in civil society [...] is normally not orientated to the state at all. The 'good citizen' may be socially active through involvement in trade unions, charitable work, community action or in any number of causes, but this does not involve a conscious rallying around the constitutional achievements of the liberal-democratic state." (Wilde 2007, p. 60)

If Habermas's understanding of solidarity is truly as misguided as Wilde suggests, then his whole theory of supranational democracy in Europe would fall, because it rests very much on the formation of this solidarity among European citizens.

Wolfgang Streeck (2014) who engaged in a debate with Habermas about his vision on Europe and how to solve the problems that emerged in Europe with the euro crisis, raised doubt whether the radical changes that Habermas proposed for European institutions could actually be performed within these institutions. In his view, the implementation of Habermas's proposals would amount to a "new re-founding of Europe" that would involve turning "the supranational institutions that have grown up in Europe upside down by revolutionary decisions made within their confines" (Streeck 2014, 217). He voiced strong doubts that these changes could come out from these institutions – "as if what is and what has come about had no meaning for what is to grow out of it in the future" (Streeck 2014, 217). In this perspective, the structures of European institutions are so strongly set that it would be rather difficult to initiate the revolutionary changes that Habermas has in mind from within these institutions. Streeck (2014, 219) therefore suggested not to surrender the social protections guaranteed by nation-states to the jurisdiction of a supranational democracy, because it could result in the emergence of a "neoliberal-supranational Leviathan."

Parker's (2009) criticism of Habermas's conception of a European supranational democracy is centered on the tension that exists between the ethical closure that Habermas seemed to advocate as a prerequisite for the emergence of social solidarity on European level, on one side, and his broader Kantian ideals of cosmopolitanism, on the other side. Parker (2009, p. 392) pointed out that it is difficult or near impossible to do both at the same time, build a European democratic community of solidaristic citizens and hold on to the ideal of a "Kantian cosmopolitanism based on a discourse ethic, which is universal and global" (Parker 2009, p. 392). Against this backdrop the term "*European* cosmopolitanism" therefore appeared "oxymoronic" to Parker (2009, p. 402). He also pointed out that Habermas's "notion of constitutional legitimacy or patriotism itself relies on some notion of affiliation if it is to be legitimate. This involves a cultural closure, a defining of self and other, insiders and outsiders." (Parker 2009, p. 396)

He especially took exception to Habermas's critique of the 2003 US invasion of Iraq and to Habermas's distinction between the "core" of the EU and its "periphery" (Parker 2009, p. 398-400). To avoid any misunderstandings, it needs to be said that Parker did not defend this war. But he charged Habermas and Derrida, the French philosopher who had co-signed the article concerned, with the othering of the US in an attempt to constitute a common European identity. "The differences Habermas notes between Europe and the US are overdrawn and constantly risk 'orientalising' an egoistic, religious, unilateral, consumerist American other and reifying a democratic, secular, solidaristic Europe." (Parker 2009, p. 399) Parker saw a similar tendency of othering where Habermas proposed a Europe of different speeds and singled out the then soon to become new member countries of the EU, because the citizens there had not internalized the historical lessons of nation-states' abuses of power that occurred during the 20th century and therefore not drawn the conclusions that would bring them to embrace a more cosmopolitan vision.

Vlad F. Perju (2018, p. 50) was rather skeptical of Habermas's dual sovereignty thesis because it treated the "national and supranational levels as co-original and co-determinate." He rejected this thesis for several reasons, but mainly because of the "asymmetry between the national and the supranational identities" that would necessarily emerge for the citizens of these two levels in favor of the nation-state. In Perju's (2018, p. 51) view, the emergence of this asymmetry was inevitable, because "by assuming that constitutional states are nation-states, the account under review undercuts what Habermas himself identifies as the urgent task of using the republican legacy of nation-states to devise mechanisms of democratic will-formation at the supranational level." In other words, Habermas designed dual sovereignty in a way that (probably inadvertently) gave preference to the nation-state level. Perju (2018, p. 72) reads Habermas's appeal to constitutional patriotism as an "invocation of national identity as constitutional doctrine" of a particular kind. He also pointed to rulings of constitutional courts, particularly the German Constitutional Court, which found in favor of the protection of national identity against transgressions from the outside. "The principle makes the European legal order derivative of national law, rather than co-original. And that derivative nature is no accident; it is normatively continuous with the logic of constitutional identity." (Perju's 2018, p. 73) This lop-sided relation between the national and the supranational level in favor of the former would create all manner of problems for the European project and allow the nation-state to "routinely undermine the project of European unification, in ways inconsistent with dual sovereignty's own normative premises" (Perju 2018, p. 51). For this reason, the expectation of a heterarchical relationship between the two levels of sovereignty was misdirected; and a hierarchy would necessarily emerge between the nation-state and European level. Perju (2018, p. 74) comes to the conclusion that the shortcomings of the dual sovereignty thesis which are rooted in Habermas preference for the constitutional state understood as nation-state would require to search for "different and, as it happens, bolder – accounts of supranational constituent power." That would be accounts that place supranational constituent power not "alongside national constituent power" (Perju 2018, p. 75).

In this section, it was shown that there is virtually no aspect of Habermas's approach which did not come under critical scrutiny. Some of Habermas's critics viewed his proposals as out of touch with the realities of globalization and of neoliberal capitalism and therefore rejected these ideas. Others saw them as too far-reaching and as threatening to the existing order which is based on the nation-state. Taking in account all these critical responses it can be said that Habermas deserves credit for provoking all these reactions and initiating a debate that shed light on the possible trajectories which the process of European integration could take in the future.

Conclusion

An aspect that has been missed in all the critical responses to Habermas's conception of a federal Europe is the defensive nature of his approach. Whereas the defense of the social state against the attacks by the neoliberal forces of globalization is a necessity, there is no path forward beyond the status quo of the social state which Habermas's theory of a supranational European democracy would specify in any way. In fact, the language that Habermas used in this context sometimes appears to indicate that he may be ready to accept a reduced version of the social state. While Habermas criticized tendencies towards globalization and their effects on the welfare state, he expressed his hope that increased European cooperation may be able to slow down the imposition of social cuts that have recently been administered in many of the EU member states. His affirmative mention of "minimal social standards" (Habermas 2001, p. 13) in this context suggests that a somewhat leaner welfare state would satisfy him, provided that it could be established at the European level through deeper European integration. His reference to European citizens who are "prepared to defend the core of a welfare state that is the backbone of a society still oriented towards social, political and cultural inclusion" (Habermas 2001, p. 9) points in the same direction.

Reacting to Streeck's (2013) book, in which the author warned of a looming economic crisis, Habermas (2013, p. 61) realized in astonishment that Streeck – as a countermeasure to this crisis – preferred withdrawing into the nation-state to the "democratic expansion of a union that had stopped halfway." Habermas (2013, p. 62) called this a "nostalgic option" that will be of little help "in the face of the epochal transformation of nation states," which are now "embedded in globalized markets." He rejected Streeck's warning that deeper European integration could lead into "repressive centralization," which, according to Habermas (2013, p. 69), is an exaggerated fear that is fed by the "false assumption" that "the institutional deepening of the European Union must result in a kind of European federal republic." Habermas reiterated that the federal state was not the model he had in mind: "Because the conditions of democratic legitimation are also met by a supranational, but *above state-level* democratic community that allows *common governance*." (Habermas 2013, p. 69)

Parker (2009) has pointed out that Habermas's distinction between "core" and "periphery" runs the risk of offending and alienating those who are grouped as belonging to the periphery. It may be added that moving forward with the process of European integration at different speeds could lead to a situation where the states that initially remained on the fringes are subject to compulsion to act. The advancement of a "core" Europe could therefore also be understood by these states as pressure to make a decision to either join the core or to endure the negative consequences associated with staying on the fringes. The advancement of a core Europe can therefore not only lead to a positive pull effect (as

Müller-Doohm suggested) but also to a situation laden with negative compulsion.

In Habermas's texts on Europe, it is sometimes not entirely clear in which order things are supposed to happen in the process of creating a supranational European democracy. Do the institutional changes come first, or is it necessary to start with the generation of a European public sphere which then provides the institutional framework for the debates about the necessary changes and influences the respective decisions; or are these two processes meant to occur simultaneously – mutually influencing and reinforcing each other? These questions arise because in some accounts Habermas stresses that an institutional reform may work as a catalyst for the democratization of Europe; in other texts he proclaims the need for a European public sphere and a transnational debate in that sphere on European politics followed by a referendum as a precondition for these institutional changes to have democratic legitimacy. The idea that a European *demos* could emerge from democratic institutional changes which work as a catalyst for this foundational process places a lot of trust in the rationality of this process and in the actors involved in it. It is true that "territorial and political integration have invariably preceded the creation of stable national identities" (Verovšek 2012, p. 367), but this does not guarantee a positive outcome of the changes suggested by Habermas, that is, that it would result in a polity which is normatively based on constitutional patriotism. Habermas may be overly optimistic about the prospects of a further federalization and democratization of the EU. But optimism is a necessary feature of visionary thinking.

Chapter 9

Conclusion

The process of European economic integration has spanned several decades since the establishment of the ECSC in 1952. This first step of regional integration in Europe marked a shift toward cooperation and supranationalism. Since then, the process of integration was joined by a large number of new member states and has deepened significantly. In this book the treaties of the EC/EU were analyzed with a focus on the political-economic environment in which they were negotiated and adopted and with a view to the social and economic impacts of their implementation. This involved considerations of the ideological influences on the integration process over time and the potential future trajectories of this process.

The founding of the ECSC signaled the beginning of a cooperative relationship between former enemies and the construction of a liberal order that supplanted the imperialist paradigm in European politics that had resulted in several wars. By encouraging intra-European competition and outlawing discriminatory practices in the production of coal and steel, the ECSC proved that shared interests might prevail over national ones, foster economic progress, and further European integration. With the Treaty of Rome and the foundation of the EEC, ordoliberalism became a strong ideological influence in this process. It especially affected the competition law of the EU, and its influence can still be felt in the EU's current competition laws. The Treaty of Rome did very little regarding social policy and left member states primarily in charge in this policy field, which also was a significant result of ordoliberal influence. As a result, social policy continued to receive little attention within the EU to date.

Ideologically, European economic integration was based on a compromise between German ordoliberalism and French dirigisme, which is why ordoliberal concepts were not fully implemented. There are divergent opinions in the literature regarding the degree of ordoliberalism's influence due to the diverse ideological forces that shaped the Treaty of Rome (Havertz 2020; Warlouzet 2019; Wigger 2017). To learn more about the opposing forces of dirigisme and ordoliberalism, future studies on European integration should look into the directives provided to the French and German delegations by the governments during the negotiations of the Treaty of Rome. Such research promises to provide further clues regarding the strengths of the major ideological influences.

It was interesting to see how the process of integration had been reinvigorated with the SEA of 1986, after the EC experienced a significant slowdown in this process in the mid-1960s and the early 1980s as a result of the oil crisis and the Empty Chair Crisis. This treaty brought about crucial institutional changes that revitalized integration. It provided a legal gateway for the creation of the EU and was essential for promoting economic cooperation within the EC. One of the key developments brought about by the SEA was the mutual recognition of national standards, which eased intra-EC trade significantly, since it lessened the need to harmonize national legislation and removed non-tariff barriers to trade. In its promotion of mutual recognition of national standards, the EC relied on landmark decisions of the ECJ such as the Dassonville Case and the Cassis de Dijon case. This essentially resulted in a situation where goods that were traded in one member country were permitted to be traded in all of them. It did, however, reflect differing member state views on the speed and breadth of the integration process and failed to resolve a number of issues, including budgetary concerns and the free movement of persons. The Schengen Agreement, which established this type of freedom across the EU, had already been concluded but not been effective at the time when the SEA came into force. It was included in the body of the treaties only much later with the Treaty of Amsterdam.

The 1992 Maastricht Treaty established the EU and prepared the introduction of the euro. It created the ECB to regulate monetary policy, preventing member states from pursuing independent monetary policies. This inability of the member states to react independently to economic shocks became problematic during the euro crisis. The EU's strict separation of monetary and fiscal policies was exposed as a fundamental design flaw of the euro. Since then, position papers from the Juncker Commission have advocated for closer fiscal integration within the EU. The adoption of a large relief fund during the Covid-19 crisis demonstrates that fiscal integration at the European level is indeed possible. It is now clear that integrating fiscal policy can improve EU stability. Politicians and economists who had previously supported a stability union are now more receptive to fiscal cooperation and the coordination of monetary and fiscal policy. Providing the EU with greater fiscal responsibility does not necessarily mean that such responsibility would have to be given up on the national level. It could rather be said that shared responsibilities between the national and supranational levels are both desirable and feasible. This is a field where further integration can be expected, since convergence in the fields of fiscal and monetary policy is essential for the EU's political unification.

Further changes to the institutional framework and decision-making procedures of the EU were made by the Amsterdam Treaty of 1999. With the impending EMU and the anticipated enlargement of the EU by a larger number of countries further modifications of the treaties were needed. The amendments concerned the powers of the EP and the ECJ, which were increased for both of these institutions. The additional powers provided to the EP were supposed to mitigate the democratic deficit in the EU. Among other things, the empowerment of the EP included the ability to approve the candidate for President of the Commission. Moreover, it gave member nations more freedom to collaborate in particular policy areas. It also transferred issues like immigration, refugee protection, and border control from the third to the first pillar of the EU, which meant that they were now administered according to the community method (as opposed to the intergovernmental method). The community method involves more supranational decision-making power than the intergovernmental method, especially concerning the involvement of the EP in that process. Despite these modifications, a number of academics believed that the Treaty of Amsterdam lacked substance, especially because it did not make any progress on the reweighting of votes in the Council, which was essential for the impending admission of states from Central and Eastern Europe (Guggenbühl 1998; Moravscik and Nicolaidis 1998). The Treaty of Amsterdam placed a strong emphasis on member states working together on employment matters, but this change was not supported by significant budgetary support for such common action. The employment-related clauses of the treaty were criticized for being inadequate and devoid of specific actions to advance employment (Guggenbühl 1998).

The divisions in the EU on important policy matters were reflected in the opt-outs which few countries made use of in the context of this treaty. With the incorporation of the Schengen Agreement into EU legislation, the Treaty of Amsterdam involved the codification of the free movement of people within the territory of the EU and the associated non-EU states that were part of that agreement. However, the United Kingdom and Ireland chose to opt-out from the Agreement. The United Kingdom had initially also opted-out from the Social Chapter. But this decision was reversed when Tony Blair became the prime minister of the United Kingdom. As a result, the United Kingdom put a significant number of labor directives into effect. The Treaty of Amsterdam resulted in a large number of smaller changes. In the literature, it has often been described as the least consequential of all the treaties of the EU (ibid.). It can be viewed as transitional, acting as a link between the more important Treaties of Maastricht and Nice, given the absence of noteworthy advances.

In 2004, the EU saw its biggest round of admissions in its history, with ten new member states (NMS) – mostly from Eastern and Central Europe – joining the bloc. In order to facilitate the accession of the new members, the negotiations of the Treaty of Nice focused on the preparedness for this event by reorganizing EU institutions such as the European Commission, the Council, and the European Parliament. Whereas significant changes were made regarding the reweighting of voting rights in the Council and the allocation of seats for each member country in the EP, the intended changes concerning the European Commission were only partly achieved with the reduction of the number of commissioners for the larger countries to one.

The research in this book found that the admission of the NMS greatly aided their economic progress, as measured in strong GDP growth. It was the increase in trade and foreign direct investment brought about by EU membership that contributed to this economic growth. Another important factor in this integration process was the substantial subsidies made by the EU to the NMS through regional and agricultural funds. While living standards have generally improved in the NMS, there are still significant economic differences in the EU between old member states and the NMS as well as between the North-West and South of the EU. As a result, it is recommended here that cohesion funds be increased with an emphasis on raising living standards and competitiveness in the NMS and the bloc's southern area.

The practice of distinguishing certain regions of the EU as "core" and "periphery" has been criticized by the author of the current study (Havertz 2014). This core-periphery distinction may involve the notion of a hierarchy in intra-EU relations, which has to be avoided in theory and practice. Jürgen Habermas has used this distinction in the measure that he has taken of the Lisbon Treaty and its contribution to the advancement of European integration. It could be argued that this distinction may alienate states on the fringes, since advancing a "core" Europe – as suggested by Habermas (2016) – could pressure these states to conform with the policy choices pertaining to this development. Habermas was disappointed with the advances of the integration process brought about by the Lisbon Treaty. His positions on this process were examined in this study. Habermas' idea of a federal Europe was challenged, emphasizing his defensive stance on welfare protections in the face of neoliberal globalization. The case could be made that Habermas does not offer a clear way out of the current social state status quo and that, based on his terminology, he might be open to a less expansive welfare state that results from closer European integration. Habermas raised questions regarding the rationality of the process when he said that institutional improvements could serve as a catalyst for democratization. He also promoted the development of a European public sphere as an essential feature of a supranational democracy in Europe. It was found that Habermas may be overly optimistic about further EU federalization and democratization.

The process of European integration was identified as a key factor for the prosperity and pacification of the continent in the period after the Second World War to date. The simultaneous pursuit of these two major goals by the EC/EU has produced ample evidence that they are mutually reinforcing. Supranationalism and interdependence are deeply entrenched in the EU. This was shown with the process of Brexit and the painstakingly difficult process of the disentanglement of Britain from the EU. But Brexit has also shown that a reversal of the integration process is possible – at a high cost. When we raise the question where the process of European integration is going and whether a further deepening is possible, we may take a look at recent developments with the response of the EU on the Covid-19 crisis. This is where the EU moved toward further fiscal integration and precipitated movement in an area where the bloc until recently appeared to allow no flexibility. The unification of fiscal policy might represent a substantial step toward deeper integration of the EU.

Previously Published Chapters

CH 2. Supranationalism and Interdependence in Europe

Havertz, Ralf. 2019. Supranationalism and Interdependence as Guarantors of Peace in Europe: The Case of the European Coal and Steel Community. *Journal of Global Politics*, 12(1), pp. 1-17. DOI: 10.35773/JGP.2019.12.1.1

CH 3. Ordoliberalism as Early Ideational Influence on European Economic Integration

Havertz, Ralf. 2020. Ordoliberalism as Early Ideational Influence on European Economic Integration. *Journal of Global Politics*, 13(1), pp. 23-46. DOI: http://dx.doi.org/10.35773/JGP.2020.13.1.23

CH 5. Maastricht and the Prospects of Fiscal Integration in the European Union

Havertz, Ralf. 2021. Maastricht and the Prospects of Fiscal Integration in the European Union. *Journal of Contemporary European Studies*. 39(2), pp. 189-226. DOI: 10.17052/jces.2021.39.2.189

CH 7. The Nice Treaty and the Integration of the New Member States of Central and Eastern Europe in the European Union

Havertz, Ralf. 2022. The Nice Treaty and the Integration of the New Member States of Central and Eastern Europe in the European Union. *Journal of Global Politics*, 15(2), pp. 119-151. DOI: https://doi.org/10.35773/JGP.2022.15.2.119

CH 8. The Constitution of Europe and Supranational Democracy

Havertz, Ralf: The Constitution of Europe and Supranational Democracy: Jürgen Habermas's Vision of the European Union. *Journal of European Union Studies*, 58 (June 2021), pp. 247-296. DOI: http://dx.doi.org/10.18109/jeus.2021.58.247

References

CH 1. Introduction

Barroso, Jose Manuel. 2007. Barroso: European Union is "non-imperial empire." Euractiv, https://www.youtube.com/watch?v=-I8M1T-GgRU.

Bonefeld, Werner. 2019. Ordoliberalism, European Monetary Union and State Power. *Critical Sociology*, 45(7–8), pp. 995-1010. DOI: https://doi.org/10.1177/0896920519832994

Devrim, Deniz and Evelina Schulz. 2009. Enlargement Fatigue in the European Union: From Enlargement to Many Unions. Elcano Royal Institute, Working Paper 13/2009, March 10, 2009, https://media.realinstitutoelcano.org/wp-content/uploads/2021/11/wp13-2009-devrim-schulz-enlargement-european-union.pdf

Secretariat of the European Round Table for Industry [ERT]. 2024. Single Market Obstacles. https://ert.eu/wp-content/uploads/2024/02/Single-Market-Compendium-of-obstacles-13-Feb-2024.pdf.

Fontaine, Pascal. 2000. A New Idea for Europe. The Schuman Declaration – 1950-2000. Second edition. https://op.europa.eu/en/publication-detail/-/publication/32543d91-caf5-45f5-9f57-c811db2c5e21.

Haas, Ernst. 1958. *The Uniting of Europe: Political, Social and Economic Forces, 1950-1957.* Stanford: Stanford University Press.

Havertz, Ralf. 2020. Ordoliberalism as Early Ideational Influence on European Economic Integration. *Journal of Global Politics*, 13(1), pp. 23-46. DOI: http://dx.doi.org/10.35773/JGP.2020.13.1.23

Her Majesty's Government. 2016. The Best of Both Worlds: The United Kingdom's Special Status in a Reformed European Union. https://assets.publishing.service.gov.uk/media/ 5a75c1dd40f0b6488c78eb82/54284_EU_Series_No1_Web_Accessible.pdf.

Hien, Josef and Christian Joerges. 2018. Dead Man Walking: Current European Interest in the Ordoliberal Tradition. Working Paper LAW 2018/03, European University Institute, Department of Law, https://cadmus.eui.eu/bitstream/handle/1814/51226/LAW_2018_03.pdf?sequence=1&isAllowed=y.

Kramer, Mark. 1999. Ideology and the Cold War. *Review of International Studies*, 25, pp. 539–576.

Nedergaard, Peter. 2013. The Influence of Ordoliberalism on European Integration Processes. MPRA Paper 52331, https://mpra.ub.uni-muenchen.de/52331/1/MPRA_paper_52331.pdf.

Nedergaard, Peter. 2019. The ordoliberalisation of the European Union? *Journal of European Integration.* Online first: DOI: https://doi.org/10.1080/07036337.2019.1658751.

Sedelmeier, Ulrich. 2024. Is there an East–West divide on democracy in the European Union? Evidence from democratic backsliding and attitudes towards rule of law interventions. *Journal of European Public Policy,* 31(3), pp. 825-849, DOI: 10.1080/13501763.2023.2198569

Schoeller, Magnus G. and Sebastian Heidebrecht. 2024. Continuity despite crises: Germany's euro policy in the light of the pandemic, war and inflation. *Journal of European Public Policy,* 31(9), pp. 2509-2533. DOI: 10.1080/13501763.2023.2218883

Warlouzet, Laurent 2019. The EEC/EU as an Evolving Compromise between French Dirigism and German Ordoliberalism (1957–1995). *Journal of Common Market Studies,* 57(1), pp. 77-93. DOI: https://doi.org/10.1111/jcms.12817

CH 2. Supranationalism and Interdependence in Europe

Alter, Karen J. and David Steinberg. 2007. The Theory and Reality of the European Coal and Steel Community. *The Roberta Buffett Center for International and Comparative Studies,* Northwestern University, Working-Paper No. 07-001, https://buffett.northwestern.edu/documents/working-papers/Buffett_07-001_Alter_Steinberg.pdf. (accessed April 2, 2019)

Archer, Clive. 2000. *The European Union. Structure and Process.* Third Edition, London: Continuum.

Berger, Michael. 2013. Motives for the foundation of the ECSC. *Poznan University of Economics Review,* 13(3), pp. 55-90.

Burgess, Michael. 2011. Entering the Path of Transformation in Europe. The Federal Legacy of the Schuman Declaration. *French Politics, Culture & Society,* 29(2), pp. 4-18.

Calaprice, Alice, Daniel J. Kennefick, and Robert Schulmann. 2015. *An Einstein Encyclopedia.* Princeton University Press.

Calingaert, Michael. 1996. *European Integration Revisited. Progress, Prospects, and U.S. Interests.* Boulder: Westview Press.

Carrel, Paul and Michael Nienaber. 2018. Merkel, Macron back euro zone budget in 'new chapter' for bloc. *Reuters,* June 19, 2018, https://www.reuters.com/article/us-germany-france-eurozone/merkel-macron-back-euro-zone-budget-in-new-chapter-for-bloc-idUSKBN1JF1L8. (accessed on June 17, 2019)

Chira-Pacanut, Constantin. 2014. Discreet Players: Jean Monnet, Transatlantic Networks and Policy-Makers in International Co-operation. *Journal of Common Market Studies*, 52(6), pp. 1242-1256.

Chryssochoou, Dimitris N. 2001. *Theorizing European Integration.* London: Sage Publications.

community_paris_18_april_1951-en-11a21305-941e-49d7-a171-ed5be548cd58.html. (accessed March 31, 2019)

Einstein, Albert. 1947. Atomic War or Peace. *The Atlantic Monthly*, November 1947, https://www.theatlantic.com/magazine/archive/1947/11/atomic-war-or-peace/305443/. (accessed March 23, 2019)

Gillingham, John. 2003. *European Integration 1950-2003. Superstate or New Market Economy?* Cambridge: Cambridge University Press.

Groenendijk, Nico. and Gert-Jan Hospers. 2002. A Requiem for the European Coal and Steel Community (1952-2002). *De Economist*, No. 150, pp. 601-612.

Grotewold, Andreas. 1973. West Germany's Economic Growth. *Annals of the Association of American Geographers*, 63(3), pp. 353-365.

Haas, Ernst. 1958. *The Uniting of Europe: Political, Social and Economic Forces, 1950-1957.* Stanford: Stanford University Press.

Holland, Martin. 1993. *European Integration. From Community to Union.* London: Pinter Publishers.

Jovanovic, Miroslav N. 2005. *The Economics of European Integration. Limits and Prospects.* Cheltenham: Edward Elgar.

Koehane, Robert and Joseph Nye. 1977. *Power and Interdependence: World Politics in Transition.* Boston: Little, Brown, and Company.

Koehane, Robert. 1989. Neoliberal Institutionalism: A Perspective on World Politics. In: Koehane, Robert. *International Institutions and State Power: Essays in International Relations Theory.* Boulder: Westview Press, pp. 1-20.

Martin, Stephen. 2004. *Coal and Steel: First Steps in European Market Integration.* February 2004, https://krannert.purdue.edu/faculty/smartin/vita/EI5060D.pdf. (accessed March 26, 2019)

Milward, Alan S. 1984. *The Reconstruction of Europe, 1945-51.* London: Methuen.

Moravcsik, Andrew. 2013. Did Power Politics Cause European Integration? Realist Theory Meets Qualitative Methods. *Security Studies*, 22, pp. 773-790.

Piodi, Franco. 2010. From the Schuman Declaration to the Birth of the ECSC: The Role of Jean Monnet. *Cordac Journals*, (6), May 2010, pp. 13-51.

Scheingold, Stuart. A. 1971. Domestic and International Consequences of Regional Integration, In: Lindberg, Leon N. and Stuart A. Scheingold (eds.), *Regional Integration: Theory and Research*, Cambridge: Harvard University Press, pp. 374-398.

Schuman, Robert. 2010. The Schuman Declaration 9 May 1950, Paris, Salon de L'Horloge, Quai D'Orsay. In: Piodi, Franco. From the Schuman Declaration to the Birth of the ECSC: The Role of Jean Monnet. *Cordac Journals*, (6), May 2010, pp. 9-11.

Treaty Establishing the European Coal and Steel Community [ECSC] (n.d.), https://www.cvce.eu/obj/treaty_establishing_the_european_coal_and_steel_

Ver Loren van Themaat, Pieter. 1994. The Dialectic Relationship between Institutional Law and Substantive Tasks in and after the Treaty of Maastricht: Some Lessons from Henry G. Schermers and Jean Monnet. In: Curtin, Deirdre M. and Tom Heukels (eds.), *Institutional Dynamics of European Integration, Essays in Honour of Henry G. Schermers*. Dordrecht: Kluwer Academic Publishers, Vol. 2, pp. 3-21.

Waltz, Kenneth N. 1959. *Man, the State, and War*. New York: Columbia University Press.

CH 3. Ordoliberalism as Early Ideational Influence on European Economic Integration

Akman, P. 2012. *The Concept of Abuse in EU Competition Law and Economic Approaches*. Oxford: Hart Publishing.

Akman, P. and Kassim, H. 2010. Myths and Myth-Making in the European Union: The Institutionalization and Interpretation of EU Competition Policy. *Journal of Common Market Studies*, 48(1), pp. 111-132.

Amable, B, and Hanké, B. 2001. Innovation and Industrial Renewal in France in Comparative Perspective. *Industry and Innovation*, 8(2), pp. 113–133.

Ban, C. 2012. Heinrich von Stackelberg and the Diffusion of Ordoliberal Economics in Franco's Spain. *History of Economic Ideas*, 20(3), pp. 137-157.

Behrens, P. 2014. The "Consumer Choice" Paradigm in German Ordoliberalism and its Impact upon EU Competition Law. Europa-Kolleg Hamburg, Institute for European Integration, Discussion Paper No1/14.

Bonefeld, W. 2012. Freedom and the Strong State: On German Ordoliberalism, *New Political Economy*, 17(5), pp. 633-656.

Bonefeld, W. 2017a. Authoritarian Liberalism: From Schmitt via Ordoliberalism to the Euro, *Critical Sociology*, 45(4+5), pp. 747-761.

Bonefeld, W. 2017b. *The Strong State and the Free Economy*. London: Rowman and Littlefield.

Bruff, I. 2017. Cease to Exist? The European 'Social' Model and the Hardening of 'Soft' EU Law. In: Tansel, Cemal Burak (ed.). *States of Discipline. Authoritarian Neoliberalism and the Contested Reproduction of Capitalist Order*. London, Rowman and Littlefield, pp. 149-169.

Candeias, M., Oberndorfer L., and Steckner A. 2014. Refounding Europe? Strategic Orientations. Rosa Luxemburg Stiftung, https://www.rosalux.de/ fileadmin/rls_uploads/pdfs/engl/rls-online_europe-has-a-different-future_nd.pdf. (accessed February 23, 2020)

Cardwell, P. J. and Snaith, H. 2018. "There's a Brand New Talk, but it's Not Very Clear": Can the Contemporary EU Really be Characterized as Ordoliberal? *Journal of Common Market Studies*, 56(5), pp. 1053-1069.

Consolidated Version of the Treaty on the Functioning of the European Union (2012) Eur-Lex, https://eur-lex.europa.eu/LexUriServ/LexUriServ.do?uri=CELEX-:12012E/ TXT:EN:PDF. (accessed March 4, 2020)

Dullien, S. and Guérot, U. 2012. The Long Shadow of Ordoliberalism: Germany's Approach to the Euro Crisis. *European Council of Foreign Relations*, https://www.ecfr.eu/page/-/ECFR49_GERMANY_BRIEF.pdf. (accessed March 27, 2020)

Erhard, L. and Müller-Armack, A. (eds.). 1972. Soziale Marktwirtschaft. Ordnung der Zukunft. Manifest '72. Frankfurt am Main: Ullstein Verlag.

Eucken, W. 1989. What kind of economic and social system? In: Peacock, A. and Willgerodt, H. (eds.) *Germany's Social Market Economy: Origins and Evolution*. London: MacMillan, pp. 27-45.

Eucken, W. 2004. *Grundsätze der Wirtschaftspolitik*. Tübingen: Mohr Siebeck.

Eucken, W. 2012a. Die Entwicklung des ökonomischen Denkens. In: Walter-Eucken-Archiv (ed.). *Wirtschaftsmacht und Wirtschaftsordnung. Londoner Vorträge zur Wirtschaftspolitik und zwei Beiträge zur Antimonopolpolitik,* Münster: Lit Verlag, pp. 65-77.

Eucken, W. 2012b. Das Problem der Wirtschaftlichen Macht. In: Walter-Eucken-Archiv (ed.). *Wirtschaftsmacht und Wirtschaftsordnung. Londoner Vorträge zur Wirtschaftspolitik und zwei Beiträge zur Antimonopolpolitik.* Münster: Lit Verlag, pp. 9-22.

Eucken, W. 2012c. Überlegungen zum Monopolproblem. In: Walter-Eucken-Archiv (ed.). *Wirtschaftsmacht und Wirtschaftsordnung. Londoner Vorträge zur Wirtschaftspolitik und zwei Beiträge zur Antimonopolpolitik.* Münster: Lit Verlag, pp. 79-84.

European Commission. 1966. Ninth General Report on the Activities of the Community. http://aei.pitt.edu/30812/1/67243_EEC_9th.pdf. (accessed February 12, 2020)

Fouskas, V. K. 2018. Neoliberalism and ordoliberalism: a critique of two forms of imperialism and authoritarianism. *Critique*, 46(3). pp 397-421.

Gerber, D. J. 1998. *Law and Competition in Twentieth Century Europe: Protecting Prometheus*. Oxford: Oxford University Press.

Hamm, W. 1989. The Welfare State at Its Limits. In: Peacock, A. and Willgerodt, H. (eds.) *Germany's Social Market Economy: Origins and Evolution*. London: MacMillan, pp. 171-194.

Havertz, R. 2019. Right-Wing Populism and Neoliberalism in Germany: The AfD's Embrace of Ordoliberalism, *New Political Economy*, 24(3), pp. 385-403.

Hecker, C. 2011. Soziale Marktwirtschaft und Soziale Gerechtigkeit – Mythos, Anspruch und Wirklichkeit. *Zeitschrift für Wirtschafts- und Unternehmensethik*, 12(2), pp. 269-294.

Hecker, C. 2014. Die Soziale Marktwirtschaft als Ausdruck bürgerlicher Werte und Lebensformen: Mentalitätsgeschichtliche und institutionenökonomische Überlegungen zum bundesdeutschen Wirtschaftsmodell der Nachkriegszeit. *Zeitschrift für Wirtschafts- und Unternehmensethik*, 15(1), pp. 110-142.

Joerges, C. and Rödl, F. 2004. "Social Market Economy" as Europe's Social Model. EUI Working Paper LAW, No 2004/8. European University Institute, https://cadmus.eui.eu/bitstream/handle/1814/2823/law04-8.pdf. (accessed February 28, 2020)

Löffler, B. 2003. *Soziale Marktwirtschaft und administrative Praxis: Das Bundeswirtschaftsministerium unter Ludwig Erhard*. Stuttgart: Franz Steiner Verlag (*Vierteljahresschrift für Sozial- und Wirtschaftsgeschichte*, Vol. 162, Supplement).

Montalban, M., Ramirez-Perez, S., and Smith A. 2011. Competition Policy Revisited: Economic Doctrines Within European Political Work. Working Paper 2011-33, Group de Recherche en Économie Théoretique et Appliquée, Université Montesquieu Bordeaux IV.

Moszynski, M. 2015. Ordoliberalism and the Macroeconomic Policy in the Face of the Euro Crisis. *Equilibrium*, 10(4), pp. 41-58.

Müller-Armack, A. 1947. *Wirtschaftslenkung und Marktwirtschaft*, Hamburg: Verlag für Wirtschaft und Sozialpolitik.

Müller-Armack, A. 1978. The Social Market Economy as an Economic and Social Order. *Review of Social Economy*, 36(3), pp. 325-331.

Müller-Armack, A. 1981. *Genealogie der Sozialen Marktwirtschaft. Frühschriften und weiterführende Konzepte*. Second expanded edition, Bern: Haupt Verlag.

Nedergaard, P. 2013. The Influence of Ordoliberalism on European Integration Processes. MPRA Paper 52331, https://mpra.ub.uni-muenchen.de/52331/1/ MPRA_paper_52331.pdf. (accessed February 21, 2020)

Nedergaard, P. 2019. The ordoliberalisation of the European Union? *Journal of European Integration*. Online first: https://doi.org/10.1080/07036337.2019.1658751. (accessed February 23, 2020)

Nedergaard, P. and Snaith, H. 2015. "As I drifted on a River I Could Not Control." The Unintended Ordoliberal Consequences of the Eurozone Crisis. *Journal of Common Market Studies*, 53(5), pp. 1094-1109.

Nozick, R. 1974. *Anarchy, State, and Utopia*, New York, NY: Basic Books.

Ptak, R. 2016. Das Staatsverständnis im Ordoliberalismus. Eine theoriegeschichtliche Analyse mit aktuellem Ausblick. In: Biebricher, T. (ed.) *Der Staat des Neoliberalismus*. Baden-Baden: Nomos, pp. 31-73.

Röpke, W. 1962. Epochenwende. In: Röpcke, Wilhelm: *Wirrnis und Wahrheit, Ausgewählte Aufsätze*. Zürich: Eugen Rentsch Verlag, pp. 105–124.

Ryner, M. 2015. Europe's ordoliberal iron cage: critical political economy, the euro crisis and its management. *Journal of European Public Policy*, 22(2), pp. 275-294.

Sally, R. 1996. Ordoliberalism and the Social Market: Classical Political Economy from Germany. *New Political Economy*, 1(2), pp. 233-254.

Somek, A. 2015. Authoritarian Liberalism. *Austrian Law Journal*, 2(1), pp. 67-87.

Sotiris, P. 2017. The Authoritarian and Disciplinary Mechanism of Reduced Sovereignty in the EU: The Case of Greece. In: Tansel, C. B. (ed.) *States of Discipline. Authoritarian Neoliberalism and the Contested Reproduction of Capitalist Order*. London, Rowman and Littlefield, pp. 171-187.

Spannagel, D. 2018. Dauerhafte Armut und verfestigter Reichtum, WSI-Bericht 2018. WSI Report No. 43/2018, https://www.boeckler.de/pdf/p_wsi_report_43_2018.pdf. (accessed February 17, 2020)

Treaty Establishing the European Economic Community (German Version). 1957. Eur-Lex, https://eur-lex.europa.eu/legal-content/DE/TXT/PDF/?uri=CELEX-:11957E/ TXT&from=EN. (accessed March 17, 2020)

Vanberg, V. 2001. Constitutionally constrained and safeguarded competition in markets and politics. In: Vanberg, Viktor, *The Constitutionality of Markets. Essays in political economy*. London: Routledge, pp. 1-16.

Walters, W. and Haahr, J. H. 2005. *Governing Europe: Discourse, Governmentality and European Integration*. London: Routledge.

Warlouzet, L. 2019. The EEC/EU as an Evolving Compromise between French Dirigism and German Ordoliberalism (1957–1995). *Journal of Common Market Studies*, 57(1), pp. 77-93.

Wigger, A. 2008. *Competition for Competitiveness: The Politics of the Transformation of the EU Competition Regime*. Doctoral Thesis, University of Amsterdam, https://research.vu.nl/ws/portalfiles/portal/42180088/8237.pdf. (accessed March 4, 2020)

Wigger, A. 2017. Debunking the Myth of the Ordoliberal Influence on Post-war European Integration. In: Hien, J. and Joerges, C. (eds.) *Ordoliberalism, Law and the Rule of Eco-*

nomics. Oxford: Hart Publishing, pp. 161-177.

Wilks, S. and McGowan, L. 1996. Competition Policy in the European Union: Creating a Federal Agency? In: Doern, G. B. and Wilks, S. (eds.) *Comparative Competition Policy: National Institutions in a Global Market*. Oxford: Clarendon Press, pp. 225-267.

Willgeroth, H. and Peacock, A. 1989. German Liberalism and Economic Revival, In: Peacock, A. and Willgerodt, H. (eds.) *Germany's Social Market Economy: Origins and Evolution*. London: MacMillan, pp. 1-14.

Wörsdörfer, M. 2010. On the Economic Ethics of Walter Eucken, In: Konrad Adenauer Stiftung (ed.) *60 Years of Social Market Economy. Formation, Development and Perspectives of a Peacemaking Formula*. Sankt Augustin: Konrad Adenauer Stiftung, pp. 20-41.

Young, B. 2014. German Ordoliberalism as Agenda Setter for the Euro Crisis: Myth Trumps Reality. *Journal of Contemporary European Studies*, 22(3), pp. 276-287.

CH 4. The Single European Act

Allen, David. 1992. European Union, the Single European Act and the 1992 programme. In: Dennis Swann (Ed.). *The Single European Market and Beyond: A Study of the Wider Implications of the Single European Act*. Routledge: London, pp. 22-42.

Berman, George A. 1989. The Single European Act: A Constitution for the Community? *Columbia Journal of Transnational Law*, 27, pp. 529-587.

Caraffini, Paolo. 2015. De Gaulle, the "Empty Chair Crisis" and the European Movement. *Perspectives on Federalism*, 7(2), DOI:10.1515/pof-2015-0014.

Craig, Paul P. and Gráinne de Búrca. 2003. *EU Law: Text, Cases and Materials*. Third edition, Oxford, New York: Oxford University Press.

Dabrowski, Marek. 2023. European Single Market: The Unfinished Business. *EconPol Forum*, 24(5), pp. 14-18.

European Commission. 1985. Completing the Internal Market. White Paper from the Commission to the European Council. Publications Office of the European Union, June 8, 1985, https://op.europa.eu/en/publication-detail/-/publication/de6e9bed-bb51-456d-9830-b12debb83019/language-en/format-PDF/source-search.

European Court of Justice [ECJ]. 1974. Procureur du Roi (Public Prosecutor) v Benoit and Gustave Dassonville. Case 8/74, Judgement of July 11, 1974, https://eur-lex.europa.eu/legal-content/EN/TXT/PDF/?uri=CELEX:61974CJ0008.

European Court of Justice [ECJ]. 1979. Rewe-Zentral AG v Federal Monopoly Administration for Spirits (Bundesmonopolverwaltung für Branntwein), Case 120/78, Judgement of February 20, 1979, https://eur-lex.europa.eu/legal-content/EN/TXT/ PD-

F/?uri=CELEX:61978CJ0120.

European Union. n.d. Customs. https://european-union.europa.eu/priorities-and-actions/actions-topic/customs_en#:~:text=The%20EU%20Customs%20Union%2C% 20established,citizens%2C%20animals%20and%20the%20environment.

Good, Kathryn. 1988. Institutional Reform Under the Single European Act. *American University International Law Review*, 3(1), pp. 299-322.

Grin, Gilles. 2020. The Negotiations on the Single European Act. In: Michael Gehler, and Wilfried Loth (Eds.). *Reshaping Europe: Towards a Political, Economic and Monetary Union, 1984-1989*. Baden-Baden: Nomos.

Hanson, Brian T. 1998. What Happened to Fortress Europe?: External Trade Policy Liberalization in the European Union. *International Organization*, 52(1), pp. 55–85.

Holmes, Peter. 1991. Non-Tariff Barriers. In: George McKenzie, and Anthony J. Venables (Eds.). *The Economics of the Single European Act*. London: Palgrave MacMillan, pp. 27-50.

Keohane, Robert O. and Stanley Hoffmann. 1991. Institutional Change in Europe in the 1980s. In: Keohane, Robert O. and Stanley Hoffmann (Eds.). *The New European Community: Decisionmaking and Institutional Change*, Boulder: Westview Press, pp. 1-39.

Micossi, Stefano. 2016. 30 Years of the Single European Market. Bruges European Economic Policy Briefings, 41/2016, https://www.coleurope.eu/sites/default/files/research-paper/beep41_0.pdf.

Moravcsik, Andrew. 1991. Negotiating the Single European Act: national interests and conventional statecraft in the European Community. *International Organization*, 45(1), pp. 19-56.

Potter, Barbara C. 1993. Implications of the Single European Act on European Community Law-Making: A Modest Step Forward. *Vanderbilt Journal of Transnational Law*, 26(2), pp. 249-269.

Single European Act [SEA] 1987. *Official Journal of the European Communities*, June 29, 1987, Document No L 169, https://eur-lex.europa.eu/resource.html?uri=cellar:a519205f-924a-4978-96a2-b9af8a598b85.0004.02/DOC_1&format=PDF.

Swann, Dennis. 1992. Standards, procurement, mergers and state aids. In: Dennis Swann (Ed.). *The Single European Market and Beyond: A Study of the Wider Implications of the Single European Act*. Routledge: London, pp. 44-66.

Thirion, Elodie. 2017. EU single market: Boosting growth and jobs in the EU. European Parliamentary Research Service. November 2017, https://www.europarl.europa.eu/RegData/etudes/BRIE/2017/611009/ EPRS_BRI%282017%29611009_EN.pdf.

Treaty establishing the European Economic Community. 2015. CVCE, University of Luxembourg, http://www.cvce.eu/obj/treaty_establishing_the_european_economic_ community_rome_25_march_1957-en-cca6ba28-0bf3-4ce6-8a76-6b0b3252696e.html.

Warlouzet, Laurent. 2020. Completing the Single Market: The European Parliament and Economic Integration, 1979-1989. European Parliamentary Research Service, April 2020, https://www.europarl.europa.eu/RegData/etudes/STUD/2020/646120/ EPRS_STU(2020)646120_EN.pdf.

Zimmermann, Hubert, and Andreas Dür (Eds.). 2016. *Key Controversies in European Integration*. Second Edition, London: Palgrave.

CH 5. Maastricht and the Prospects of Fiscal Integration in the European Union

Arestis, P. and Sawyer, M. 2011. The Design Faults of the Economic and Monetary Union. Journal of Contemporary European Studies, 19(1), pp. 21-32.

Beck, T. and Kotz, H.-H. 2017. Banking union: Rules versus discretion? In: Beck, T and Kotz H.-H. (eds.) Ordoliberalism: A German Oddity? London: CEPR Press, pp. 107-119.

Bonefeld, W. 2017. The Strong State and the Free Economy, London: Rowman & Littlefield.

Boonstra, W. 2010. How EMU can be strengthened by central funding of public deficits. ELEC, Cahier Comte Boël, (14) April 2010, pp. 3-14.

Boonstra, W. 2011. Saving EMU. Central funding of public deficits, combined with a renewed Stability and Growth Pact, can stabilize the eurozone. Rabobank Working Paper Series, No. 2011/02, January 2011, https://economics.rabobank.com/globalassets/documents/ 2011/januari/wp1102wbo_central_funding_emu_fund.pdf. (accessed January 29, 2022).

Chazan, G. 2020. Coronavirus crisis prompts German rethink on Eurobonds. Some say country's traditional resistance to debt mutualisation could crumble. Financial Times, April 6, 2020, 2020 from https://www.ft.com/content/8da39299-b257-4e8f-9b83-a84a8930f1c1. (accessed January 29, 2022)

Clark, D. 2020. Viewpoint: Managing euro zone sovereign risk in the face of the pandemic. IPE News, August 21, 2020, https://www.ipe.com/viewpoint-managing-euro-zone-sovereign-risk-in-the-face-of-the-pandemic/10047379.article. (accessed January 29, 2022)

De Grauwe, P. and Ji, Y. 2017. Making the Eurozone Sustainable by Financial Engineering or Political Union? Journal of Common Market Studies, 57 (Annual Review), pp. 40-48.

De Grauwe, P. and Ji, Y. 2018. Core-Periphery Relations in the Eurozone, The Economists' Voice, 15(1), https://eprints.lse.ac.uk/91328/1/De-Grauwe_Core-periphery.pdf. (accessed September 20, 2024)

De Grauwe, P. and Moesen, W. 2009. Gains for All: A Proposal for Common Euro Bonds. Intereconomics, May/June 2009, pp. 132-135.

Delfs, A., Nussbaum, A. and Kuzmanovic, J. 2020. Merkel Offers Breakthrough Deal to Shield EU From Virus Fallout. Bloomberg, May 18, 2020, https://www.bloomberg.com/news/articles/2020-05-18/merkel-offers-breakthrough-deal-to-shield-eu-from-virus-fallout. (accessed January 29, 2022)

Delors, J. 1989. Report on economic and monetary union in the European Community. Presented April 17, 1989 by the Committee for the Study of Economic and Monetary Union, http://aei.pitt.edu/1007/1/ monetary_delors.pdf. (accessed January 29, 2022)

Delpla, J. and von Weizsäcker, J. 2010. The Blue Bond Proposal. Breugel Policy Briefs, Issue 2010 (3), May 2010, https://www.bruegel.org/wp-content/uploads/imported/ publications/1005-PB-Blue_Bonds.pdf. (accessed January 29, 2022)

Dullien, S. and Guérot, U. 2012. The Long Shadow of Ordoliberalism: Germany's Approach to the Euro Crisis. European Council of Foreign Relations, February 2012, https://www.ecfr.eu/page/-/ECFR49_GERMANY_BRIEF.pdf. (accessed January 29, 2022)

Enderlein, H., Bofinger, P., Piris, J.-C., de Grauwe, P., Rodrigues, M. J., Pisani-Ferry, J., Sapir, A., and Vitorino, A. 2012. Completing the Euro. A road map towards fiscal union in Europe. Report of the 'Tomaso Padoa-Schioppa Group,' Paris: Notre Europe.

European Central Bank [ECB]. n.d.-a. Single Supervisory Mechanism. https://www.bankingsupervision.europa.eu/about/thessm/html/index.en.html. (accessed September 20, 2024)

European Central Bank [ECB]. n.d.-b. Banking Union. https://www.bankingsupervision.europa.eu/about/bankingunion/html/index.en.html. (accessed January 29, 2022)

European Commission. 2017. Reflection Paper on the Deepening of the Economic and Monetary Union, May 2017, https://ec.europa.eu/commission/sites/beta-political/files/reflection-paper-emu_en.pdf. (accessed January 19, 2021)

European Commission. 2018. Frequently asked questions: Enabling framework for sovereign bond-backed securities. May 24, 2018, https://ec.europa.eu/commission/presscorner/detail/en/MEMO_18_3726. (accessed January 29, 2022)

European Commission. 2020. SURE, The European instrument for temporary Support to mitigate Unemployment Risks in an Emergency (SURE). https://ec.europa.eu/info/business-economy-euro/economic-and-fiscal-policy-coordination/financial-assistance-eu/funding-mechanisms-and-facilities/sure_en. (accessed January 29, 2022)

European Council. 2020. COVID-19: the EU's response to the economic fallout. December 15, 2020, https://www.consilium.europa.eu/en/policies/coronavirus/covid-19-economy/ (accessed January 29, 2022).

European Systemic Risk Board [ESRB]. 2018. Sovereign Bond-backed Securities: A Feasibility Study, Volume II: Technical Analysis. January 2018, https://www.esrb.europa.eu/pub/pdf/reports/esrb.report180129_sbbs_volume_II_technicalanalysis~99341e199d.en.pdf?8f11ae128257fd62a97bde6ffd258bd5. (accessed January 29, 2022)

Feld, L. P., Köhler, E., and Nienstedt, D. 2017. The 'Dark Ages of German macroeconomics' and other alleged shortfalls in German economic thought. Beck T. and Kotz H.-H. (eds.) Ordoliberalism: A German Oddity? London: CEPR Press, pp. 41-51.

Hacker, B. 2013. On the Way to a Fiscal or a Stability Union? The Plans for a 'Genuine' Economic and Monetary Union. Friedrich-Ebert-Stiftung, December 2013, https://library.fes.de/pdf-files/id/ipa/10400.pdf. (accessed January 29, 2022)

Hacker, B. and Koch, C. M. 2017. The divided Eurozone. Mapping Conflicting Interests on the Reform of the Monetary Union. Friedrich-Ebert-Stiftung, http://library.fes.de/pdf-files/bueros/bruessel/13335.pdf. (accessed January 29, 2022)

Havertz, R. 2013. Prospects of Common Debt Responsibility in the Euro Area. The Case for Eurobonds. Journal of International Studies, 19, April 2013, pp. 57-90.

Havertz, R. 2014. The Making of the European Periphery: A Critical Analysis of the Discourse on the Euro Crisis. The 21Century Political Science Review, 24(3), pp. 711-736.

Isenson, N. 2012. Merkel: No eurobonds 'as long as I live.' Deutsche Welle, June 27, 2012, https://www.dw.com/en/merkel-no-eurobonds-as-long-as-i-live/a-16052083. (accessed January 29, 2022)

Juncker, J.-C. and Tremonti, G. 2010. E-bonds would end the crisis. Financial Times, December 5, 2010.

Juncker, J.-C., Tusk, D., Dijsselbloem, J., Draghi, M., and Schulz, M. 2015. Completing Europe's Economic and Monetary Union, European Commission. https://ec.europa.eu/commission/sites/beta-political/files/5-presidents-report_en.pdf. (accessed January 19, 2021)

Leandro, Á. and Zettelmeyer, J. 2019. Creating a Euro Area Safe Asset without Mutualizing Risk (Much). Peterson Institute for International Economics, August 2019, https://papers.ssrn.com/sol3/papers.cfm?abstract_id=3432533. (accessed January 29, 2022)

McKinnon, R. I. 1963. Optimum Currency Areas. American Economic Review, 52(4), pp. 717-725.

Mongelli, F. P. 2008. European Economic and Monetary Integration and the Optimum Currency Area Theory, European Commission. Directorate-General for Economic and Financial Affairs, Economic Papers 302, February 2008, https://ec.europa.eu/economy_finance/publications/pages/publication12081_en.pdf. (accessed January 29, 2022)

Mundell, R. A. 1961. A Theory of Optimum Currency Areas. The American Economic Review, 51(4), pp. 657-665.

Myrus, R. 1994. From Bretton Woods to Brussels: A Legal Analysis of the o Brussels: A Legal Analysis of the Exchange-Rate Arrangements of the International Monetary Fund and the European Community. Fordham Law Review, 62(7), pp. 2095-2124.

Nedergaard, P. 2013. The Influence of Ordoliberalism on European Integration Processes. MPRA Paper 52331, 2013, https://mpra.ub.uni-muenchen.de/52331/1/ MPRA_paper_52331.pdf. (accessed January 29, 2022)

Nienaber, M. 2020. Update 1 – German minister rejects euro bonds – 'It's a phantom debate." Reuters, March 23, 2020, https://www.reuters.com/article/health-coronavirus-germany-eurobonds/update-1-german-minister-rejects-euro-bonds-its-a-phantom-debate-idUSL8N2BG8RK. (accessed January 29, 2022)

Pobrić, N. 2019. Is the Idea of the Common Eurobonds Issuance in the Eurozone Sustainable? InterEuLawEast, 6(2), pp. 1-30.

Šehović, D. 2014. Coordination of Monetary and Fiscal Policy in the European Monetary Union. Management, 19(73), pp. 69-83.

Skalkos, D. P. 2018. The Sensitive Swings of the European Pendulum: Ordoliberal and Neo-Keynesian Competitive Theories of European Integration. Bulgarian Economic Papers No. 06-2018, May 2018, Center for Economic Theories and Policies, Sofia University, https://www.uni-sofia.bg/index.php/eng/content/download/194439/1333121/file/BEP-2018-06.pdf. (accessed January 29, 2022)

Thomadakis, A. 2020. Will Covid-19 Reduce the Resistance to Eurobonds? ECMI Event Report, European Capital Markets Institute, April 2, 2020, https://www.ecmi.eu/sites/default/files/eurobonds_-_event_summary_0.pdf. (accessed January 29, 2022)

Treaty Establishing the European Economic Community (German Version). 1957. Eur-lex, https://eur-lex.europa.eu/legal-content/DE/TXT/PDF/?uri=CELEX:11957E/TXT&from=EN. (accessed January 29, 2022)

Treaty on European Union. 1992. Council of the European Communities and Commission of the European Communities. https://europa.eu/european-union/sites/europaeu/files/ docs/body/treaty_on_european_union_en.pdf. (accessed January 8, 2021)

Von der Burchard, H. 2020. Merkel backs EU bonds to fight coronavirus crisis. Politico, April 20, 2020, https://www.politico.eu/article/coronavirus-angela-merkel-eu-bonds/. (accessed January 29, 2022)

Werner Report. 1970. Report to the Council and the Commission on the Realisation by Stages of Economic and Monetary Union in the Community. Supplement to Bulletin 11 (1970) of the European Communities, from https://ec.europa.eu/economy_finance/publications/pages/publication6142_en.pdf. (accessed January 29, 2022)

Wyplosz, C. 2011. Eurobonds: Concepts and Applications, Directorate General for Internal

Policies, Department A: Economic and Scientific Policies, Eurobonds: Concepts and Implications. March 2011, pp. 5-16, https://www.europarl.europa.eu/document/ activities/cont/201103/20110316ATT15710/20110316ATT15710EN.pdf. (accessed January 29, 2022)

Young, B. 2017. Ordoliberalism as an 'irritating German idea.' Beck, T. and Kotz, H.-H. (eds.) Ordoliberalism: A German Oddity? London: CEPR Press, pp. 31-40.

CH 6. The Treaty of Amsterdam

Bär, Stefani, Thomas Gehring, Ingmar von Homeyer, R. Andreas Kraemer, Anne-Gabrielle Mazurek, Anneke Klasing, and Richard G. Tarasofky. 2000. Closer Co-operation, a new instrument for European Environmental Policy? *European Integration online Papers*, 4(13), http://eiop.or.at/eiop/texte/2000-013a.htm.

Burrows, Noreen. 2010. Equal pay for work of equal value. http://www.era-comm.eu/oldoku/SNLLaw/05_Equal_Pay/2010_09_Burrows_EN.pdf.

Cerny, Phlipp G. and Mark Evans.1999. New Labour, Globalization, and the Competition State. Center for European Studies, Working Paper Series, No. 70, https://ces.fas.harvard.edu/uploads/files/Working-Papers-Archives/CES_WP70.pdf.

Due, Ole. 1998. The Amsterdam Treaty and the Court of Justice. February 1998, https://ciaotest.cc.columbia.edu/wps/duo01/.

European Commission. 1997. Facts about the "Social Chapter." Memo/97/13, February 5, 1997, https://ec.europa.eu/commission/presscorner/api/files/document/print/en/

European Commission. 1999a. Entry Into Force of the Amsterdam Treaty on 1 May. https://ec.europa.eu/commission/presscorner/api/files/document/print/en/ip_99_269/IP_99_269_EN.pdf.

European Commission. 1999b. Treaty of Amsterdam: What Has Changed in Europe. https://aei.pitt.edu/15098/1/MOVE-TREATYOFAMSTERDAM-1999.pdf.

Goetschy, Janine and Philippe Pochet. 1997. The Treaty of Amsterdam: A new approach to employment and social affairs? *Transfer*, (3) (November 1997), pp. 607-620.

Guggenbühl, Alain. 1997. A Contemplative View on the First Pillar of the New European Union. *Eipascope*, (2). pp. 1-5.

Havertz, Ralf. 2022. The Nice Treaty and the Integration of the New Member States of Central and Eastern Europe in the European Union. *Journal of Global Politics*, 15(2), pp. 119-151,

Huysmans, Jef. 2000. The European Union and the Securitization of Migration. *Journal of Common Market Studies*, 38(5), pp. 751–77.

Jessop, Bob. n.d. From Thatcherism to New Labour: Neo-Liberalism, Workfarism, and Labour Market Regulation. Department of Sociology, Lancaster University, https://www.lancaster.ac.uk/fass/resources/sociology-online-papers/papers/jessop-from-thatcherism-to-new-labour.pdf

memo_97_13/MEMO_97_13_EN.pdf

Moravscik, Andrew and Kalypso Nicolaidis. 1998. Federal Ideals and Constitutional Realities in the Treaty of Amsterdam. *Journal of Common Market Studies*, 36 (Annual Review), pp. 13-38.

Moravscik, Andrew and Kalypso Nicolaidis. 1999. Explaining the Treaty of Amsterdam: Interests, Influence, Institutions. *Journal of Common Market Studies*, 37(1), pp. 59-85.

Nentwich, Micheal and Gerda Falkner. 1997. The Treaty of Amsterdam: Towards a New Institutional Balance. *European Integration online Papers*, 1(15), http://eiop.or.at/eiop/texte/1997-015a.htm.

Piris, Jean-Claude and Giorgio Maganza. 1998. The Amsterdam Treaty: Overview and Institutional Aspects. *Fordham International Law Journal*, 22(6), pp. S32-S47.

Pollack, Mark A. 2000. A Blairite Treaty: Neo-Liberalism and Regulated Capitalism in the Treaty of Amsterdam. In: Neunreither, Karlheinz and Antje Wiener (Eds.). *European Integration After Amsterdam: Institutional Dynamics and Prospects for Democracy.* Oxford University Press, pp. 266–289.

Spruyt, Hendrik and Lucy Lyons. 2000. *The Development of the European Union*. New York: Columbia University Press.

Stubb, Alexander C.-G. 1998. The Amsterdam Treaty and Flexible Integration. *European Community Study Association (ECSA) Review*, 11(2), pp.1-5.

Treaty establishing the European Economic Community. 2015. CVCE, University of Luxembourg, http://www.cvce.eu/obj/treaty_establishing_the_european_economic_community_rome_25_march_1957-en-cca6ba28-0bf3-4ce6-8a76-6b0b3252696e.html.

Treaty of Amsterdam amending the Treaty on Europe Union, the Treaties establishing the European Communities and certain related acts [Treaty of Amsterdam]. 1997. *Official Journal C 340*, pp. 1-144. https://eur-lex.europa.eu/legal-content/EN/TXT/PDF/?uri=CELEX:11997D/TXT.

CH 7. The Nice Treaty and the Integration of the New Member States of Central and Eastern Europe in the European Union

Baas, Timo and Herbert Brückner. 2011. EU Eastern Enlargement: The Benefits from Integration and Free Labour Movement. *CESifo, DICE Report*, (2), pp. 44-51.

Breitenfellner, Andreas, Jesus Crespo Cuaresma, Peter Mooslechner, and Doris Ritzberger-Grünwald. 2008. The Impact of EU Enlargement in 2004 and 2007 on FDI and Migration Flows. Gravity Analysis of Factor Mobility. *Monetary Policy & the Economy*, (2), pp. 101-120.

Buchholz, Katharina. 2020. Which Countries are EU Contributors and Beneficiaries? Statista, 13 January 2020. https://www.statista.com/chart/18794/net-contributors-to-eu-budget/. (accessed July 1, 2022)

D'Auria, Francesca, Kieran Mc Morrow, and Karl Pichelmann. 2008. Economic impact of migration flows following the 2004 EU enlargement process: A model based analysis. European Commission, Directorate-General for Economic and Financial Affairs, Economic Papers 349, November 2008. https://ec.europa.eu/economy_finance/publications/pages/publication13389_en.pdf. (accessed July 6, 2022)

Edjaharian, Vérane. 2013. Article 16 [The Council]. In: Blanke, Hermann-Josef and Stelio Mangiameli (eds.). *The Treaty on European Union (TEU). A commentary*. Berlin: Springer, pp. 645-680.

European Commission. 2003. Summary of the Treaty of Nice. https://ec.europa.eu/commission/presscorner/api/files/document/print/en/memo_03_23/MEMO_03_23_EN.pdf. (accessed June 28, 2022)

European Commission. 2006. Enlargement, two years on: all win as new Member States get richer. https://ec.europa.eu/commission/presscorner/detail/mt/IP_06_557. (accessed June 29, 2022)

European Commission. 2014. Evolution of agricultural income as a share of average income in the economy. https://www.agronewscastillayleon.com/sites/default/files/docs/articulos/ graph3_en.pdf. (accessed July 4, 2022)

European Commission. 2021a. CAP expenditure in the total EU expenditure. October 2021. https://ec.europa.eu/info/sites/default/files/food-farming-fisheries/farming/documents/ cap-expenditure-graph1_en.pdf. (accessed July 3, 2022)

European Commission. 2021b. CAP expenditure and CAP reform path. October 2021. https://ec.europa.eu/info/sites/default/files/food-farming-fisheries/farming/documents/ cap-expenditure-graph2_en.pdf. (accessed July 3, 2022)

European Commission. 2021c. European Farm Economics Overview. https://ec.europa.eu/info/sites/default/files/food-farming-fisheries/farming/documents/ eu-farm-econ-overview-2018_en.pdf. (accessed July 4, 2022)

European Commission. 2021c. Evolution of agricultural income as a share of average income in the economy. September 2021. https://ec.europa.eu/info/sites/default/files/food-farming-fisheries/farming/documents/cap-expenditure-graph4_en.pdf. (accessed July 4, 2022)

European Parliament. 2015. Implementation of the First Pillar of the CAP 2014-2020 in the

EU Member States. Directorate-General for Internal Policies. https://www.europarl.europa.eu/RegData/etudes/STUD/2015/563386/IPOL_STU(2015)563386_EN.pdf. (accessed July 4, 2022)

European Parliament. 2022. The Common Agricultural Policy in figures. April 2022. https://www.europarl.europa.eu/ftu/pdf/en/FTU_3.2.10.pdf. (accessed July 4, 2022)

Eurostat. 2022a. GDP per capita, consumption per capita and price level indices. https://ec.europa.eu/eurostat/statistics-explained/index.php?title=GDP_per_capita,_ consumption_per_capita_and_price_level_indices#Overview. (accessed July 4, 2022)

Eurostat. 2022b. Employment and activity by sex and age - annual data. https://ec.europa.eu/ eurostat/databrowser/view/lfsi_emp_a/default/table?lang=en. (accessed July 5, 2022)

Eurostat. 2022c. Unemployment rates by sex, age and citizenship (%). https://ec.europa.eu/eurostat/databrowser/view/lfsa_urgan/default/table?lang=en. (accessed July 6, 2022)

Eurostat. 2022d. Immigration by age and sex. https://ec.europa.eu/eurostat/databrowser/view/migr_imm8/default/table?lang=en. (accessed July 6, 2022)

Eurostat. 2022e. Emigration by age and sex. https://ec.europa.eu/eurostat/databrowser/view/migr_emi2/settings_1/table?lang=en. (accessed July 6, 2022)

Felbermayr, Gabriel, Jasmin Gröschl, and Thomas Steinwachs. 2018. The Trade Effects of Border Controls: Evidence from the European Schengen Agreement. *Journal of Common Market Studies*. 56(2), pp. 335-351.

Freeman, Daan, Gerdien Meijerink, and Rutger Teulings (2022). Trade benefits of the EU and the Internal Market. CBP Bureau for Economic Policy Analysis. January 2022. https://www.cpb.nl/sites/default/files/omnidownload/CPB-Communication-Trade-benefits-of-the-EU-and-the-Internal-Market.pdf. (accessed December 9, 2022)

Georgescu, Vladimir. 2014. Patterns in Trade in Selected European Union Countries. "Ovidius" University Annals, Economic Sciences Series, 14(1), pp. 125-130.

Henke, Roberto, Theo Benos, Fabrizio De Filippis, Mara Giua, Fabio Pierangeli, and Maria Rosaria Pupo D'Andrea. 2018. The New Common Agricultural Policy: How do Member States Respond to Flexibility? *Journal of Common Market Studies*, 56(2), pp. 403-419.

House of Commons. 2000. The "Amsterdam Triangle." Select Committee on Foreign Affairs, Sixth Report. https://publications.parliament.uk/pa/cm199900/cmselect/cmfaff/384/38404.htm. (accessed July 1, 2022)

Incaltarau, Cristian, Gabriela Carmen Pascariu, and Neculai-Cristian Surubaru. 2020. Evaluating the Determinants of EU Funds Absorption across Old and New Member States – the Role of Administrative Capacity and Political Governance. *Journal of Common*

Market Studies, 58(4), pp. 941–961.

Johnson, Debra. 2005. Developments in the Economies of the New Member States and the Candidate Countries. *Journal of Common Market Studies*, 43(Annual Review), pp. 199–214.

Kahanec, Martin and Klaus F. Zimmermann. 2009. Migration in an Enlarged EU: A Challenging Solution? European Commission, Directorate-General for Economic and Financial Affairs, Economic Papers 363, March 2009. https://ec.europa.eu/economy_finance/publications/pages/publication14287_en.pdf. (accessed July 6, 2022)

KucCzarnecka, Marta, Andrea Saltelli, Magdalena Olczyk, and Erik Reinert (2021). The opening of Central and Eastern European countries to free trade: A critical assessment. Economic Dynamics, 58, September 2021, pp. 23-24.

Mussa, Giorgio. 2022. The European Commission. European Parliament, May 2022, https://www.europarl.europa.eu/factsheets/en/sheet/25/the-european-commission. (accessed June 30, 2022)

Official Journal. 1997. Consolidated Version of the Treaty establishing the European Community. *Official Journal* 40, pp. 173-306. https://eur-lex.europa.eu/legal-content/EN/TXT/PDF/?uri=OJ:C:1997:340:FULL&from=EN97/C340/03. (accessed June 30, 2022)

Official Journal. 2001. Treaty of Nice. Amending the Treaty on European Union, the Treaties establishing the European Communities and certain related acts. (Document No. 2001/C 80/01) 11 March 2001. https://eur-lex.europa.eu/legal-content/EN/TXT/PDF/?uri=CELEX:12001C/TXT&from=EN. (accessed June 30, 2022)

Official Journal. 2008. Consolidated version of the Treaty on European Union – TITLE VI: FINAL PROVISIONS – Article 48 (ex Article 48 TEU). *Official Journal* 115, pp. 41-43, http://data.europa.eu/eli/treaty/teu_2008/art_48/oj. (accessed June 29, 2022)

Official Journal. 2012. Consolidated version of the Treaty on European Union. (Document No. C 326/13) 26 October 2012, https://eur-lex.europa.eu/resource.html?uri=cellar:2bf140bf-a3f8-4ab2-b506-fd71826e6da6.0023.02/DOC_1&format=PDF. (accessed July 1, 2022)

Official Journal. 2016. Consolidated version of the Treaty on the Functioning of the European Union. (Document No. C 202/3), 7 June 2016. https://eur-lex.europa.eu/legal-content/EN/TXT/PDF/?uri=CELEX:12016E/TXT&from=EN. (accessed July 1, 2022)

Organization of Economic and Cooperation and Development [OECD]. 2020. International Migration Outlook 2020: Romania. https://www.oecd-ilibrary.org/sites/89085e47-en/index.html?itemId=/content/component/89085e47-en. (accessed July 7, 2022)

Rant, Vasja, Mojmir Mrak and Matej Marinč (2020) The Western Balkans and the EU budget: the effects of enlargement. *Southeast European and Black Sea Studies*, 20(3), pp. 431-453.

Razauskas, Tomas and Borisas Melnikas. 2009. The New Member States – The Place in the Integration Road of the EU Economy. *European Integration Studies*, 3, pp.126-133.

Rodil-Marzábal, Óscar, and Hugo Campos-Romero. 2021. The Intra-EU Value Chain: An Approach to Its Economic Dimension and Environmental Impact. *Economies*, 9(2), pp. 1-7. (accessed July 7, 2022)

Statistics Poland. 2021. Information on the size and directions of emigration for temporary stay from Poland between 2004-2020. https://stat.gov.pl/download/gfx/portalinformacyjny/en/defaultaktualnosci/3289/8/14/1/information_on_the_size_and_directions_of_emigration_for_temporary_stay_from_poland_between_2004-2020.pdf. (accessed July 7, 2022)

Tosun, Jale. 2014. New EU member states have been more effective at spending European Regional Development Funding than old member states. London School of Economics and Political Science, 14 August 2014, https://blogs.lse.ac.uk/europpblog/2014/08/14/new-eu-member-states-have-been-more-effective-at-using-european-regional-development-funding-than-old-member-states/. (accessed July 2, 2022)

United Nations. n.d. Romania. Migration Profiles. https://esa.un.org/miggmgprofiles/ indicators/files/Romania.pdf. (accessed July 7, 2022)

Zhao, Xuejiao, Chaoying Shi, and Yangjie Li (2022) Can European Union (EU) Enlargement Boost Regional Economic Common Growth? Multi-Period Difference-in-Difference (DID) Method. *Journal of Environmental and Public Health*, Article ID: 4502628. https://doi.org/10.1155/ 2022/4502628. (accessed December 10, 2022)

CH 8. The Constitution of Europe and Supranational Democracy

Auer, S. 2010. 'New Europe': Between Cosmopolitan Dreams and Nationalist Nightmares. *Journal of Common Market Studies*, 48(5), pp. 1163–1184.

Balibar, E. 2012. What Democratic Europe? A Response to Jürgen Habermas. *Social Europe Journal*, 7(1), pp. 9-11.

Breda, V. 2006. A European Constitution in a Multinational Europe or a Multinational Constitution for Europe? *European Law Journal*, 12(3), pp. 330–344.

Brunkhorst, H. 2016. Für eine Repolitisierung der europäischen Öffentlichkeit. *Blätter für deutsche und internationale Politik*, January 2016, pp. 69-76.

Grimm, D. 1995. Does Europe Need a Constitution? *European Law Journal*, 1(3), pp. 282-302.

Habermas, J. 1986. Eine Art Schadensabwicklung: Die apologetischen Tendenzen in der deutschen Zeitgeschichtsschreibung. *Die Zeit*, July 11, 1986.

Habermas, J. 1989. *The Structural Transformation of the Public Sphere. An Inquiry into a Category of Bourgeoise Society*. Trans. Thomas Burger and Frederick Lawrence, Cambridge: MIT Press.

Habermas, J. 1995. Remarks on Dieter Grimm's 'Does Europe Need a Constitution?' *European Law Journal*, 1(3), pp. 303-307.

Habermas, J. 2001. Why Europe Needs a Constitution. *New Left Review*, Vol. 11, September/October 2001, pp. 5-26.

Habermas, J. 2003a. Toward a Cosmopolitan Europe. *Journal of Democracy*, 14(4), pp. 86-100.

Habermas, J. 2003b. Europäische Identität und universalistisches Handeln. *Blätter für deutsche und internationale Politik*, July 2003, pp. 801-806.

Habermas, J. 2008a. Ein avantgardistischer Spürsinn für Relevanzen. Die Rolle des Intellektuellen und die Sache Europas. In: Habermas, J. *Ach, Europa. Kleine Politische Schriften XI*. Frankfurt am Main: Suhrkamp, pp. 77-87.

Habermas, J. 2008b. Europa und seine Immigranten. In: Habermas, J. *Ach, Europa. Kleine Politische Schriften XI*. Frankfurt am Main: Suhrkamp, pp. 88-95.

Habermas, J. 2008c. Europapolitik in der Sackgasse. Plädoyer für eine Politik der abgestuften Integration. In: Habermas, J. *Ach, Europa. Kleine Politische Schriften XI*. Frankfurt am Main: Suhrkamp, pp. 96-127.

Habermas, J. 2011. Der Konstruktionsfehler der Währungsunion. *Blätter für deutsche und internationale Politik*, May 2011, pp. 64-66.

Habermas, J. 2013. Demokratie oder Kapitalismus? *Blätter für deutsche und internationale Politik*, May 2013, pp. 59-70.

Habermas, J. 2014. 'Für ein starkes Europa' – aber was heißt das? *Blätter für deutsche und internationale Politik*, March 2014, pp. 85-94.

Habermas, J. 2015. Democracy in Europe: Why the Development of the EU into a Transnational Democracy Is Necessary and How It Is Possible. *European Law Journal*, 21(4), pp. 546–557.

Habermas, J. 2016. Für eine demokratische Polarisierung. *Blätter für deutsche und internationale Politik*, November 2016, pp. 35-42.

Habermas, J. and Derrida, J. 2003. February 15, or What Binds Europeans Together: A Plea for a Common Foreign Policy, Beginning in the Core of Europe. *Constellations*, 10(3), pp. 291-297.

Habermas, J., Fischer, J., Enderlein, H., and Callies, C. 2011. Europa und die neue deutsche Frage. *Blätter für deutsche und internationale Politik*, May 2011, pp. 85-94.

Habermas, J., Gabriel, S., and Macron, E. 2017. Europa neu Denken. *Blätter für deutsche und internationale Politik*, https://www.blaetter.de/ausgabe/2017/april/europa-neu-denken. (accessed January 30, 2022)

Havertz, R. 2014. The Making of the European Periphery: A Critical Analysis of the Discourse on the Euro Crisis. *The 21Century Political Science Review*, 24(3), pp. 711-736.

Müller-Doohm, S. 2009. Nationalstaat, Kapitalismus, Demokratie. Philosophisch-politische Motive im Denken von Jürgen Habermas. *Leviathan*, 37(4), pp. 501-517.

Parker, O. 2009. Why EU, Which EU? Habermas and the Ethics of Postnational Politics in Europe. *Constellations*, 16(3), pp. 392-409.

Perju, V. F. 2018. Double Sovereignty in Europe? A Critique of Habermas's Defense of the Nation-State. *Texas International Law Journal*, 53(1), pp. 49-75.

Rousseau, J.-J. 1968. *The social contract*, London: Penguin Books.

Scharpf, F. W. 2015. Das Dilemma der supranationalen Demokratie in Europa. *Leviathan*, Vol. 43(1), pp. 11-28.

Streeck, W. 2013. *Gekaufte Zeit: Die vertagte Krise des demokratischen Kapitalismus*. Berlin: Suhrkamp Verlag.

Streeck, W. 2014. Small-State Nostalgia? The Currency Union, Germany, and Europe: A Reply to Jürgen Habermas. *Constellations*, 21(2), pp. 213-221.

Verovšek, P. J. 2012. Meeting Principles and Lifeworlds Halfway: Jürgen Habermas on the Future of Europe. *Political Studies*, 60(2), pp. 363–380.

Wilde, L. 2007. Europe and the 're-regulation of world society': A critique of Habermas. *Capital & Class*, 31(3), pp. 47-66.

CH 9. Conclusion

Guggenbühl, Alain. 1997. A Contemplative View on the First Pillar of the New European Union. *Eipascope*, (2). pp. 1-5.

Habermas, Jürgen. 2016. Für eine demokratische Polarisierung. *Blätter für deutsche und internationale Politik*, November 2016, pp. 35-42.

Havertz, Ralf. 2014. The Making of the European Periphery: A Critical Analysis of the Discourse on the Euro Crisis. *The 21Century Political Science Review*. 24(3), pp. 711–736.

Havertz, Ralf. 2020. Ordoliberalism as Early Ideational Influence on European Economic Integration. *Journal of Global Politics*, 13(1), pp. 23-46. DOI: http://dx.doi.org/10.35773/JGP.2020.13.1.23

Moravscik, Andrew and Kalypso Nicolaidis. 1998. Federal Ideals and Constitutional Realities in the Treaty of Amsterdam. *Journal of Common Market Studies*, 36 (Annual Review), pp. 13-38.

Warlouzet, Laurent 2019. The EEC/EU as an Evolving Compromise between French Dirigism and German Ordoliberalism (1957–1995). *Journal of Common Market Studies*, 57(1), pp. 77-93. DOI: https://doi.org/10.1111/jcms.12817

Wigger, Angela 2017. Debunking the Myth of the Ordoliberal Influence on Post-war European Integration. In: Hien, Josef and Christian Joerges (eds.). *Ordoliberalism, Law and the Rule of Economics*. Oxford: Hart Publishing, pp. 161-177.

Author Biography

Ralf Havertz is a Professor of International Relations at Keimyung Adams College, Keimyung University. He is holding an M.A. in Political Science from the University of Aachen and a Ph.D. in Political Science from Free University Berlin. He wrote his doctoral dissertation about "Botho Strauß' Essay 'Anschwellender Bocksgesang' und die Neue Rechte. Eine kritische Diskursanalyse." His main research interests are in International Political Economy, European Politics, Political Sociology, and Political Theory. Recently, he has published a book on the rise of right-wing populism in Germany (Radical Right Populism in Germany. AfD, Pegida, and, the Identitarian Movement. Routledge, 2021) and a chapter in the Oxford Handbook of Ordoliberalism (2022). He has also published several articles on European integration.

Stages of European Integration

The Treaties of the European Union from a Political-Economic Perspective

Author	Ralf Havertz
First Printed	2024.12.6
First Published	2024.12.13
Director	Yeonkwan Park
Executive Contents Creator	Sunho Shin
Contents Creator	Haejung Jang Mihyun Park
Designer	Jaeyoung Choi
Published by	HANKUK UNIVERSITY OF FOREIGN STUDIES KNOWLEDGE CONTENTS & PRESS 107, Imun-ro, Dongdaemun-gu, Seoul 02450, Korea Tel.) 82-2-2173-2497 Fax.) 82-2-2173-3363 E-mail) press@hufs.ac.kr Online) http://press.hufs.ac.kr
Printed by	Twinbell Tel.) 82-2-2088-1810
ISBN	979-11-7199-276-8 [93340]
Price	26,000 Won (20USD)